THE TEACHER'S DILEMMA

Essays on School Law and School Discipline

Thomas R. McDaniel

UNIVERSITY
PRESS OF
AMERICA

For Nan, Robb, and Katy.

ACKNOWLEDGEMENTS

Many people have helped me in the publication of this volume of essays. I am grateful to James Lyons and Helen Hudson of University Press of America for their editorial support and assistance. Both Joanne Jolly and Phyllis Fagen provided excellent typing and proofreading service, and I appreciate their patience and help. I also want to acknowledge the kind support of Converse College. My colleagues on the faculty and administration have given encouragement and the Faculty Research Fund has underwritten the costs I would otherwise have had to assume myself. As always I appreciate the patience and understanding of my near and dear ones--Nan, Robb, and Katy.

CREDITS

The articles in this volume (all written by Thomas R. McDaniel) are reprinted with the permission of the following publishers:

Phi Delta Kappan for "The NTE and Teacher Certification" (vol. 59, no. 3, November, 1977); "The Teacher's Ten Commandments: School Law in the Classroom: (vol. 60, no. 10, June, 1979); "South Carolina's Educator Improvement Act: Portent of the Super School Board?" (vol. 63, no. 2, October, 1981); "Exploring Alternatives to Punishment: Keys to Effective Discipline" (vol. 61, no. 7, March, 1980).

The National Elementary Principal for "How to Weed Out Incompetent Teachers Without Getting Hauled Into Court" (vol. 59, no. 3, March, 1980).

American Secondary Education for "A Stitch in Time: Principles of Preventive Discipline" (vol. 9, no. 2, June, 1979) and "The Principal's School Law Quiz" (vol. 12, no. 2, Fall, 1982).

The Clearing House for "Corporal Punishment and Teacher Liability: Questions Teachers Ask" (vol. 54, no. 1, September, 1980); "How To Be a More Effective Authoritarian: A Back-to-Basics Approach to School Discipline" (vol. 55, no. 6, February, 1982).

Childhood Education for "Identifying Discipline Problems: A Self Evaluation Exercise" (vol. 57, no. 4, March/April, 1981). Reprinted by permission of Thomas R. McDaniel and the Association for Childhood Education International, 3615 Wisconsin Avenue, N.W., Washington, DC. Copyright 1981 by the Association.

Early Years for "Discipline--Just Another One of the Basics" (vol. X, no. 2, October, 1979). Reprinted with permission of the publisher Allen Raymond, Inc., Darien, CT 06820. This article is a retitled and revised version of "So You Want Good Classroom Behavior? Don't Preach It--Teach It!"

Orbit: Ideas About Teaching and Learning for "'Well Begun is Half Done': A School-Wide Project for Better Discipline" (vol. 13, no. 1, February, 1982).

The Educational Forum for "Power in the Classroom"

(vol. XLVI, no. 1, Fall, 1981) and "Teaching Special
Creation and Evolution in the Public Schools" (future
issue).

TABLE OF CONTENTS

INTRODUCTION

Two of the most important areas of concern for the contemporary public school are school law and school discipline. In these two (often interrelated) areas we can observe a dazzling explosion of innovations, issues, and ideas. What teacher or principal can claim to understand well the legal rights and responsibilities of educators and students? What professional educator fully comprehends the emerging legal principles governing teacher certification, corporal punishment, teacher dismissal, curriculum legitimacy, and negligence? Does any teacher not worry about classroom management, discipline problems, and student motivation?

The fact is that school law and school discipline are increasingly the issues that shape school policy and practice, at times becoming the tails that wag the educational dog. And yet until recently few educators have had the intensive study of law and discipline that educational reality demands. Indeed, it is still a rarity to find a teacher who has had a course in pupil management techniques (special educators may be exceptions) or in school law. How can teachers prevent discipline problems from occurring? How can they identify behaviors that interfere with learning? What power does (and should) a teacher have over student actions and what alternatives to legally dangerous punishment practices are available to educators?

The Teacher's Dilemma is a collection of essays that address the questions raised above. The professional educator who wants to be better informed about the principles and practices now available to public school teachers and administrators will find this examination relevant and practical. Each essay focuses on a particular aspect of school law and school discipline to illumine a given issue, its theoretical context, and its educational application.

The educator who masters the concepts and techniques explored in this volume will face the problems of school law and school discipline with renewed confidence, understanding, and competence.

THE TEACHER'S TEN COMMANDMENTS:

SCHOOL LAW IN THE CLASSROOM

In recent years public school teachers have been made painfully aware that the law defines, limits, and prescribes many aspects of a teacher's daily life. Schools are no longer protected domains where teachers rule with impunity; ours is an age of litigation. Not only are parents and students ready to use the courts for all manner of grievances against school and teacher, the growing legislation itself regulates more and more of school life. In addition to an unprecedented number of laws at all levels of government, the mind-boggling array of complex case law principles (often vague and contradictory) adds to the confusion for the educator.

The Ten Commandments of School Law described below are designed to provide the concerned and bewildered teacher with some significant general guidelines in the classroom. While statutes and case law principles may vary from state to state or judicial circuit to judicial circuit, these school law principles have wide applicability in the United States today.

Commandment 1: thou shalt not worship in the classroom

This may seem something of a parody of the Biblical First Commandment--and many teachers hold that indeed their religious freedom and that of the majority of students has been limited by the court cases prohibiting prayer and Bible reading--but the case law principles here have been designed to keep public schools <u>neutral</u> in religious matters. The First Amendment to the Constitution, made applicable by the Fourteenth Amendment to state government (and hence to public schools, which are agencies of state government), requires that there be no law "respecting the establishment of religion or prohibiting the free exercise thereof." As the Supreme Court declared in the <u>Everson</u> decision of 1947, "Neither [a state nor the federal government] can pass laws which aid one religion, aid all religions, or prefer one religion over another." Such rules, said the Court, would violate the separation of church and state principle of the First Amendment. Further, the Court argued

1

in the later <u>Schempp</u> and <u>Murray</u> decision (1963), the free exercise clause of the First Amendment "has never meant that a majority could use the machinery of the state to practice its beliefs." Finally, in that same decision about prescribed Bible reading and prayer, the Court said that "what our Constitution indispensably protects is the freedom of each of us, be he Jew or agnostic, Christian or atheist, Buddhist or freethinker, to believe or disbelieve, to worship or not to his own conscience, uncoerced and unrestrained by government."

The application of this neutrality principle to education has resulted in some of the following guidelines for public schools:

1. Students may not be required to salute the flag nor to stand for the flag salute, if this conflicts with their religious beliefs.
2. Bible reading, even without comment, may not be practiced in a public school when the intent is to promote worship.
3. Prayer is an act of worship and as such cannot be a regular part of opening exercises or other aspects of the regular school day.
4. Worship services (e.g., prayer and Bible reading) are not constitutional even if voluntary rather than compulsory. Not consensus, nor majority vote, nor excusing objectors from class or participation makes these practices legal.

On the other hand, public schools <u>may</u> offer courses in comparative religion, history of religion, the Bible as literature, etc., since these would be academic experiences rather than religious ones. "Released-time" programs during school hours for outside-of-school religious instruction have been held to be constitutional by the Supreme Court (<u>Zorach v. Clauson</u>, 1952). The constitutionality of such "gray area" practices as religious holidays and pageants (e.g., Christmas programs), silent meditation, and teaching the Genesis concept of "special creation" of man in science classes as an alternative to evolution[1] have not been clearly determined by the courts to date, but any religious program or practice is suspect in a public school.

<u>Command II: thou shalt not abuse academic freedom</u>

Under First Amendment protection, teachers are given the necessary freedom and security to use the classroom as a forum for the examination and discussion of ideas. Freedom of expression is a prerequisite for education in a democracy--and the schools, among other responsibilities, are agents of democracy. Students are citizens too, and they are also entitled to freedom of speech. As Justice Abe Fortas, who delivered the Supreme Court's majority opinion in the famous Tinker decision (1969), put it:

> It can hardly be argued that either students or teachers shed their constitutional rights at the schoolhouse gate....In our system state-operated schools may not be enclaves of totalitarianism...[and] students may not be regarded as closed-circuit recipients of only that which the state chooses to communicate.

Case law has developed over the years to define the parameters of free expression for both teachers and students:

1. Teachers may discuss controversial issues in the classroom if they are relevant to the curriculum, although good judgment is required. Issues that disrupt the educational process, are demonstrably inappropriate to the legitimate objectives of the curriculum, or are unreasonable for the age and maturity of the students may be prohibited by school officials.

2. Teachers may discuss current events, political issues, and candidates so long as neutrality and balanced consideration prevail. When teachers become advocates and partisans, supporters of a single position rather than examiners of all positions, they run the risk of censure.

3. A teacher may use controversial literature containing "rough" language but must "take care not to transcend his legitimate professional purpose" (Mailoux v. Kiley, 1971, U.S. District Court, Massachusetts). Again, courts will attempt to determine curriculum relevance, disruption of the educational process, and appropriateness to the age and maturity of the students. Reaction of parents is less important than the reaction of students. As one

decision said, "With the greatest respect to such parents, their sensibilities are not the full measure of what is proper education" (<u>Keefe</u> v. <u>Geanakos</u>, 1969, First Circuit Court).

4. Teachers and students are increasingly (but not yet universally) guaranteed <u>symbolic</u> free speech, including hair length and beards, armbands, and buttons. Courts generally determine such issues in terms of the "substantial disruption" that occurs or is clearly threatened. Male teachers may, in any event, wear beards, although school policies may require these to be neat and well-groomed (see for example, <u>Finot</u> v. <u>Pasadena City</u> Board of <u>Education</u>, 1967, U.S. District Court, California). Dress codes for students are generally allowable when they are intended to provide for health, safety, and "decency." When they exist merely to promote the "tastes" of the teacher or administration, they have usually been struck down by the courts.

5. Teachers, in short, are free to deal with controversial issues (including politics and sex) and to use controversial methods and materials if these are educationally defensible, appropriate to the students, and not "materially and substantially" disruptive. Courts use a balancing test to determine when students' and teachers' rights to academic freedom must give way to the competing need of society to have reasonable school discipline.

Commandment III: thou shalt not engage in private activities that impair teaching effectiveness

Of all the principles of school law, this commandment is probably the most difficult to delineate with precision. The private and professional areas of a teacher's life have been, for the most part, separated by recent court decisions. A mere 60 years ago teachers signed contracts with provisions prohibiting marriage, falling in love, leaving town without permission of the school board, smoking cigarettes, loitering in ice-cream stores, and wearing lipstick. But now a teacher's private life is considered his own business. Thus, for example, many court cases have established that teachers have the same citizenship rights outside the classroom as any other person does.

Teachers, however, have always been expected by

society to abide by high standards of personal conduct. Whenever a teacher's private life undermines effective instruction in the class, there is a possibility that the courts will uphold his dismissal from his job. To guard against this possibility, the teacher should consider some of the following principles:

1. A teacher may belong to any organization or association--but if he participates in illegal activities of that organization he may be dismissed from his job.
2. A teacher may write letters to newspapers criticizing school policies and his superiors--unless it can be shown that such criticism impairs morale or working relationships. In the landmark Pickering decision (1968), the Supreme Court upheld a teacher who had written such a letter but pointed out that there was in this case "no question of maintaining either discipline by immediate supervisors or harmony among co-workers...."
3. A teacher's private affairs do not normally disqualify him from teaching except to the extent that it can be shown that such affairs, as one court put it, "mar him as a teacher." If a teacher is immoral in public or voluntarily (or through indiscretion) makes known in public a private act of immorality, he may indeed be dismissed. Courts are still debating the rights of homosexual teachers, with decisions falling on both sides of this issue.
4. Laws which say that teachers may be dismissed for "unprofessional conduct" or "moral turpitude" are interpreted narrowly, with the burden of proof on the employer to show that the particular circumstances in a case constitute "unfitness to teach."
5. Whenever a teacher's private affairs include sexual involvement with students, it may be presumed that courts will declare that such conduct constitutes immorality indicating unfitness to teach.

Commandment IV: thou shalt not deny students due process

The Fourteenth Amendment guarantees citizens "due process of law" whenever the loss of a right is at stake. Since education has come to be considered such a right (a "property" right), and since students are considered to be citizens, case law in recent years has defined certain procedures to be necessary (see the

Supreme Court's 1967 <u>In Re Gault</u> case for rights of juveniles in the justice system) in providing due process in particular situations:

1. A rule that is patently or demonstrably unfair or a punishment that is excessive may be found by a court to violate the "substantive" due process of a student (see, for example, the Supreme Court's 1969 <u>Tinker</u> decision). At the heart of due process is the concept of fair play, and teachers should examine the substance of their rules and the procedures for enforcing them to see if both are reasonable, nonarbitrary, and equitable.

2. The extent to which due process rights should be observed depends on the gravity of the offense and the severity of punishment that follows. The Supreme Court's <u>Goss</u> v. <u>Lopez</u> decision (1975) established minimal due process for suspensions of 10 days or less, including oral or written notice of charges and an opportunity for the student to present his side of the story.

3. When a student is expelled from school, he should be given a statement of the specific charges and the grounds for expulsion, a formal hearing, names of witnesses against him, and a report of the facts to which each witness testifies (see the leading case, <u>Dixon</u> v. <u>Alabama State Board of Education</u>, 1961). Furthermore, it is probable that procedural due process for an expelled student gives him the right to challenge the evidence, cross-examine witnesses, and be represented by counsel. (See, for example, the New York Supreme Court's 1967 <u>Goldwyn</u> v. <u>Allen</u> decision.) Finally, such a student may appeal the decision to an impartial body for review.

It is advisable for schools to develop written regulations governing procedures for such areas as suspension, expulsion, discipline, publications, and placement of the handicapped. The teacher should be aware of these regulations and should provide his administration with specific, factual evidence whenever one of his students faces a serious disciplinary decision. The teacher is also advised to be guided by the spirit of due process--fairness and evenhanded justice--when dealing with less serious incidents in the classroom.

<u>Commandment V:</u> thou shalt not punish behavior through

academic penalties

It is easy for teachers to lose sight of the distinction between punishing and rewarding academic performance, on the one hand, and disciplinary conduct on the other. Grades, for example, are frequently employed as motivation for both study behavior and paying-attention behavior. There is a great temptation for teachers to use one of the few weapons still in their arsenal (i.e., grades) as an instrument of justice for social infractions in the classroom. While it may indeed be the case that a student who misbehaves will not perform well academically because of his conduct, courts are requiring schools and teachers to keep those two domains separate.

In particular, teachers are advised to heed the following general applications of this principle:

1. Denial of a diploma to a student who has met all the academic requirements for it but who has broken a rule of discipline is not permitted. Several cases (going back at least as far as the 1921 Iowa Valentine case) are on record to support this guideline. It is also probable that exclusion from a graduation ceremony as a punishment for behavior will not be allowed by the courts.
2. Grades should not be reduced to serve disciplinary purposes. In the Wermuth case (1965) in New Jersey, the ruling against such a practice included this observation by the state's commissioner of education: "Whatever system of marks and grades a school may devise will have serious inherent limitations at best, and it must not be further handicapped by attempting to serve disciplinary purposes too."
3. Lowering grades--or awarding zeros--for absences is a questionable legal practice. In the recent Kentucky case of Dorsey v. Bale (1975), a student had his grades reduced for unexcused absences and, under the school's regulation, was not allowed to make up the work; five points were deducted from his nine-weeks' grade for each unexcused absence. A state circuit court and the Kentucky Court of Appeals declared the regulation to be invalid. The courts are particularly likely to invalidate regulations that constitute "double jeopardy"--e.g., suspending a student for disciplinary reasons and giving him zeros while he is suspended

In general, teachers who base academic evaluation on academic performance have little to fear in this area. Courts do not presume to challenge a teacher's grades per se when the consideration rests only on the teacher's right or ability to make valid academic judgments. There have been cases, and we may expect to see more, against schools for failing to teach basic skills. Such "accountability" cases (like the Peter Doe case in California) may soon have a direct effect on grading and instructional practices.

Commandment VI: thou shalt not misuse corporal punishment

Corporal punishment is a controversial method of establishing discipline. The Supreme Court refused to disqualify the practice under a recent suit (Ingraham v. Wright, 1977) in which it was argued that corporal punishment was "cruel and unusual punishment" and thus a violation of the Constitution's Eighth Amendment. Presently, only Massachusetts and New Jersey prohibit corporal punishment in schools by state law, although Maryland bans it by state school board policy. Thirteen other states expressly permit corporal punishment, while the rest have some general provision authorizing teachers to maintain discipline.[2]

In those states not prohibiting corporal punishment, teachers may--as an extension of their in loco parentis authority--use "moderate" corporal punishment to establish discipline. There are, however, many potential legal dangers in the practice. In loco parentis is a limited, perhaps even a vanishing, concept, and teachers must be careful to avoid these misuses of corporal punishment if they want to stay out of the courtroom:

1. The punishment must never lead to permanent injury. No court will support as "reasonable" or "moderate" that physical punishment which permanently disables or disfigures a student. Many an assault and battery judgment has been handed down in such cases. Unfortunately for teachers, "accidents" that occur during corporal punishment and ignorance of a child's health problems (brittle bones, hemophilia, etc.) do not excuse a teacher for liability in most cases.

2. The punishment must not be unreasonable in

terms of the offense, nor may it be used to enforce an unreasonable rule. The court examines all the circumstances in a given case to determine what was or was not "reasonable" or "excessive."

3. The punishment must not be motivated by spite, malice, or revenge. Whenever teachers administer corporal punishment in a state of anger, they run a high risk of losing an assault and battery suit in court. Since corporal punishment is practiced as a method of correcting student behavior, any evidence that physical force resulted from a teacher's bad temper or quest for revenge is damning. On the other hand, in an explosive situation (e.g., a fight) a teacher may protect himself and use that force necessary to restrain a student from harming the teacher, others, or himself.

4. The punishment must not ignore such variables as the student's age, sex, size, and physical condition.

5. The punishment must not be administered with inappropriate instruments or to parts of the body where risk of injury is great. For example, a Texas case ruled that it is not reasonable for a teacher to use his fists in administering punishment. Another teacher lost a suit when he struck a child on the ear, breaking an eardrum. The judge noted, "Nature has provided a part of the anatomy for chastisement, and tradition holds that such chastisement should there be applied." It should be noted that creating mental anguish and emotional stress by demeaning, harassing, or humilitating a child may be construed as illegal punishment too.

6. While an earlier Supreme Court case, Baker v. Owen (1975), required procedural safeguards prior to paddling, the later Ingraham case overturned such requirements as hearings and notices in corporal punishment practices.

Courts must exercise a good deal of judgment in corporal punishment cases to determine what is "moderate," "excessive," "reasonable," "cruel," "unusual," "malicious intent," or "capricious." Some courts (e.g., in Glaser v. Marietta, 1972) have ruled that schools may not employ corporal punishment if a student's parents notify the school that they do not want it. Suffice it to say that educators should exercise great care in the use of corporal punishment.

Commandment VII: thou shalt not neglect students' safety

One of the major responsibilities of any teacher is to keep his students safe from unreasonable risk of harm or danger. The majority of cases involving teachers grow out of negligence charges relating to the teacher's failure to supervise properly in accordance with his in loco parentis obligation (to act "in place of the parents"), his contractual obligations, and his professional responsibility. While the courts do not expect teachers to protect children from "unforeseeable accidents" and "acts of God," they do require teachers to act as a reasonably prudent teacher should in protecting students from possible harm or injury.

Negligence is a tort ("wrong") that exists only when the elements of duty, violation, cause, and injury are present. A teacher is generally responsible for using good judgment in determining what steps are necessary to provide for adequate supervision of the particular students in his charge, and the given circumstances dictate what is reasonably prudent in each case. A teacher who has a duty to his students but who fails to fulfill this duty because of carelessness, lack of discretion, or lack of diligence may violate his duty with a resultant injury to a student. In this instance the teacher may be held liable for negligence as the cause of the injury to the student.

Several guidelines can help teachers avoid this all-too-common and serious lawsuit:

1. Establish and enforce rules of safety in school activities. This is particularly important for the elementary teacher, since many injuries to elementary students occur on playgrounds, in hallways, and in classroom activity sessions. The prudent teacher anticipates such problems and establishes rules to protect students from such injuries. Generally, rules should be written down, posted, and taught.

2. Be aware of school, district, and state rules and regulations as they pertain to student safety. One teacher was held negligent when a child was injured because the teacher did not know that there was a state law requiring safety glasses in a shop activity. It is also important that a teacher's own rules not

conflict with regulations at higher levels. <u>Warn</u>
students of any hazard in a room or in an instructional
activity.

3. Enforce safety rules when violations are observed. In countless cases teachers have been found
negligent when students repeatedly broke important
safety rules, eventually injuring themselves or
others, or when a teacher should have foreseen the
danger but did not act as a "reasonably prudent"
teacher would have in the same situation to correct
the behavior. One teacher observing a mumblety-peg
game at recess was held negligent for not stopping it
before the knife bounced up and put out an eye of one
of the players.

4. Provide a higher standard of supervision
when students are younger, handicapped, and/or in a
potentially dangerous activity. Playgrounds, physical
education classes, science labs, and shop classes require particular care and supervision. Instruction
must be provided to insure safety in accordance with
the children's maturity, competence, and skill.

5. Learn first aid, because a teacher may be
liable for negligence if he does not get or give
prompt, appropriate medical assistance when necessary.
While a teacher should not give children medicine, even
aspirin, he should, of course, allow any legitimate
prescriptions to be taken as <u>prescribed</u>. There should
be school policy governing such procedures.

6. Advise substitute teachers (and student
teachers) about any unusual medical, psychological,
handicapping, or behavioral problem in your class. If
there are physical hazards in your class--bare light
cords, sharp edges, loose boards, insecure window
frames, etc.--warn everyone about these too. Be sure
to report such hazards to your administration and
janitorial staff--as a "prudent" teacher would do.

7. Be where you are assigned to be. If you have
playground, hall, cafeteria, or bus duty, <u>be</u> there.
An accident that occurs when you are some place other
than your assigned station may be blamed on your
negligence, whereas if you had been there it would not
be so charged. Your responsibility for safety is the
same for extracurricular activities you are monitoring
as it is for classes.

8. If you have to leave a classroom (particularly
a rowdy one), stipulate the kind of conduct you expect
and make appropriate arrangements--such as asking
another teacher to check in. Even this may not be

adequate precaution in terms of your duty to supervise
if the students are known to be troublemakers, are
quite immature, or are mentally retarded or emotionally
disturbed. You run a greater risk leaving a science
class or a gym class than you do a social studies
class.

9. Plan field trips with great care and provide
for adequate supervision. Many teachers fail to
realize that permission notes from home--no matter how
much they disclaim teacher liability for injury--do
not excuse a teacher from providing proper supervision.
A parent cannot sign away this right of his child.
Warn children of dangers on the trip and instruct
them in rules of conduct and safety.

10. Do not send students on errands off school
grounds, because they then become your agents. If
they are injured or if they injure someone else, you
may well be held liable. Again, the younger and less
responsible the child, the greater the danger of a
teacher negligence charge. To state the obvious, some
children require more supervision than others.

Much of the advice above is common sense, but the
"reasonably prudent" teacher needs to be alert to the
many requirements of "due care" and "proper supervision." The teacher who anticipates potentially
dangerous conditions and actions and takes reasonable
precautions--through rules, instruction, warnings,
communications to superiors, and presence in assigned
stations--will do a great deal to minimize the chances
of pupil injury and teacher negligence.

Commandment VIII: thou shalt not slander or libel your students

This tort is much less common than negligence,
but it is an area of school law that can be trouble-
some, especially under the recent "Buckley Amendment."
One of the primary reasons for the Family Educational
Rights and Privacy Act (1974) was that school records
contain so much misinformation and hearsay and so
many untrue (or, at least, questionable) statements
about children's character, conduct, and morality that
access to these records by students or their parents
in order to correct false information seemed warranted.
A teacher's right to write anything about a student
under the protection of confidential files no longer
exists. Defamation of character through written

12

communication is <u>libel</u> while such defamation in oral
communication is <u>slander</u>. There are ample opportunities for teachers to commit both offenses.

Teachers are advised to be careful about what they
say about students (let alone other teachers!) to
employers, colleges, parents, and other personnel in
the school. Adhere to the following guidelines:

1. Avoid vague, derogatory terms on permanent
records and recommendations. Even if you do not
<u>intend</u> to be derogatory, value judgments about a
student's character, life-style, or home life may be
found defamatory in court. In one case, a North
Carolina teacher was found guilty of libel when she
said on a permanent record card that a student was
"ruined by whiskey and tobacco." Avoid characterizing
students as "crazy," "immoral," or "delinquent."
2. Say or write only what you know to be true
about a student. It is safer to be an objective de-
scriber of what you have observed than to draw possibly unwarranted and untrue conclusions and judgments.
The truth of a statement is strong evidence that
character has not been defamed, but in some cases
where the <u>intent</u> has been to malign and destroy the
person, truth is not an adequate defense.
3. Communicate judgments of character only to
those who have a right to the information. The teacher
has "qualified privileged communication," which means
that so long as he communicates in good faith information that he believes to be true to a person who has
reason to have this information, he is protected.
However, the slandering of pupils in a teachers'
lounge bull session is another thing altogether.
4. If a student confides a problem to you in
confidence, keep that communication confidential. A
student who is on drugs, let us say, may bring you to
court for defamation of character and/or invasion of
privacy if you spread such information about indiscrim-
inately. On the other hand, if a student confides
that he has participated in a felonious crime or gives
you information that makes you aware of a "clear and
present" danger, you are obligated to bring such
information to appropriate authorities. Find out the
proper limits of communication and the authorized
channels in your school and state.
5. As a related issue, be careful about "search
and seizure" procedures too. Generally, school lockers

13

are school property and may be searched by school officials, but to search a student--or require him to empty his pockets--probably violates the Fourth Amendment to the Constitution <u>unless</u> there exists an indication of a clear and present danger such as a bomb or weapon. Deleterious items such as drugs have also been allowable as cause for search and seizure by most courts.

Teachers need to remember that students are citizens and as such enjoy at least a limited degree of the constitutional rights that adult citizens enjoy. Not only "due process," "equal protection," and "freedom of religion" but also protection from teacher torts such as "negligence" and "defamation of character" is provided to students through our system of law. These concepts apply to all students, including those in elementary grades.

Commandment IX: thou shalt not photocopy in violation of copyright law

On January 1, 1978, the recently revised copyright law went into effect and with it strict limitations on what may be photocopied by teachers for their own or classroom use under the broad concept of "fair use." In general, "fair use" of copyrighted material means that the use should not impair the value of the owner's copyright by diminishing the demand for that work, thereby reducing potential income for the owner.

Because photocopying has become a standard practice for teachers in an era of technological wizardry, special attention should be given to the new requirements. In general, educators are given greater latitude than most other users: "Spontaneous" copying is more permissible than "systematic" copying. Students have greater latitude than teachers in copying materials.

A teacher may:

1. Make a <u>single</u> copy for his own research or class preparation of a chapter from a book; an article from a periodical or newspaper; a short story, poem, or essay; a chart, graph, diagram, cartoon, or picture from a book, periodical, or newspaper.

2. Make _multiple_ copies for classroom use only (but not to exceed one copy per student) of a complete poem, if it is fewer than 250 words and printed on not more than two pages; an excerpt from a longer poem, if it is fewer than 250 words; a complete article, story, or essay, if it is fewer than 2,500 words; an excerpt from a prose work, if it is fewer than 1,000 words or 10% of the work, whichever is less; one chart, graph, diagram, drawing, cartoon, or picture per book or periodical.

However, a teacher may _not_:

1. Make multiple copies of work for classroom use if another teacher has already copied the work for use in another class in the same school.
2. Make copies of a short poem, article, story, or essay from the same author more than once in the same term.
3. Make multiple copies from the same collective work or periodical issue more than three times a term. (The limitations in items 1-3 do not apply to current news periodicals or newspapers.)
4. Make a copy of works to take the place of anthologies.
5. Make copies of "consumable" materials such as workbooks, exercises, answer sheets to standardized tests, and the like.

When teachers make brief, spontaneous, and limited copies of copyrighted materials other than consumables, they are likely to be operating within the bounds of fair use. Whenever multiple copies of copyrighted materials are made (within the guidelines above), each copy should include a notice of the copyright. Needless to say, some schools will abuse the new law. Enforcement of the requirements will be difficult, but that does not alter the legality of photocopying practices. Actually, the new copyright provisions for educators may be considered generous. A National Education Association spokesman said, "We achieved so much more in this legislation than we expected, it is a great victory for education."

Commandment X: thou shalt not be ignorant of the law

The axiom, "Ignorance of the law is no excuse," holds as true for teachers as anyone else. Indeed, courts are increasingly holding teachers to higher standards of competence and knowledge commensurate with their higher status as professionals. Since education is now considered a right--guaranteed to black and white, rich and poor, "normal" and handicapped--the legal parameters have become ever more important to teachers in this litigious era. As one recent school law text asserts:

> Legal activism has found a home in the public schools. Not only are there more suits against teachers, there are also more types of suits against teachers. Furthermore, the educators are increasingly finding themselves in a position where they are called upon to go into court to protect themselves. Thus the teacher needs to know the extent of both rights and responsibilities not only in the classroom but in the world beyond.[3]

How, then, can the teacher become aware of the law and its implications for the classroom? Consider the following possibilities:

1. Sign up for a course in school law. If the local college or university does not offer such a course, attempt to have one developed.
2. Ask your school system administration to focus on this topic in inservice programs.
3. Tap the resources of the local, state, and national professional organizations for pertinent speakers, programs, and materials. The NEA, for example, publishes such monographs as What Every Teacher Should Know About Student Rights. Phi Delta Kappa publishes two "fast-backs" in this area, Student Discipline and the Law and The Legal Rights of Students.
4. Explore state department of education sources, since most states will have personnel and publications that deal with educational statutes and case law in your particular state.
5. Establish school (if not personal) subscriptions to professional journals. The Phi Delta Kappan, Today's Education, the Journal of Law and Education, and the Mental Disability Law Reporter are only a few of the journals that regularly have columns and/or

articles to keep the teacher aware of new developments in school law.

6. Make sure that your school or personal library includes such books as E. C. Bolmeier's Legality of Student Disciplinary Practices (Michie, 1975) and Judicial Excerpts Governing Students and Teachers (Michie, 1977), Louis Fischer and David Schimmel's The Civil Rights of Teachers (Harper & Row, 1973) and The Civil Rights of Students (Harper & Row, 1975), Rennard Strickland's Avoiding Teacher Malpractice (Hawthorn, 1976), Perry A. Zirkel's A Digest of Supreme Court Decisions Affecting Education (Phi Delta Kappa, 1978), and Patricia A. Hollander's Legal Handbook for Educators (Westview, 1978). There are many other pertinent books, of course, including those by noted authorities such as Thomas Flygare, David Rubin, Chester Nolte, and Edmund Reutter.

The better informed teachers are about their legal rights and responsibilities the more likely they are to avoid the courtroom--and there are many ways to keep informed.

My Teacher's Ten Commandments are not exhaustive, nor are they etched in stone. School law, like all other law, is constantly evolving and changing so as to reflect the thinking of the times;[4] and decisions by courts are made in the context of particular events and circumstances that are never exactly the same. But the prudent professional will be well served by these commandments if he internalizes the spirit of the law as a guide to his actions as a teacher--in the classroom, the school, and the community.

FOOTNOTES

1. For a discussion of this interesting educational and legal controversy, see my "Special Creation and Evolution in the Classroom: Old Wine in New Wineskins?," School Science and Mathematics, January, 1977, pp. 47-52.
2. For a comprehensive survey of corporal punishment practices in the various states, see Tobyann Boonin, "The Benighted Status of U.S. School Corporal Punishment Practice," Phi Delta Kappan, January, 1979, pp. 395, 396.

3. Rennard Strickland et al., Avoiding Teacher Malpractice (New York: Hawthorn Books, 1976), p. 7.
4. For a good treatment of changes and trends, see Daniel L. Duke et al., "Emerging Legal Issues Related to Classroom Management," Phi Delta Kappan, December, 1978, p. 305-09.

HOW TO WEED OUT INCOMPETENT TEACHERS

WITHOUT GETTING HAULED INTO COURT*

How do you dismiss an experienced, certified, tenured teacher who is judged to be incompetent or unfit for teaching? It's a question you may have had reason to ask yourself recently. If so, you're not alone. Faced, like you, with a surplus of teachers, a declining birth rate, Proposition 13-type cutbacks, and more aggressive and accountability-minded parents, boards of education and local school administrators throughout the country are raising the same question. And almost invariably they're finding that there's no easy solution. Existing state laws governing discharge and the more drastic step--decertification--make these processes so difficult and time consuming that few school administrators are willing or able to remove inadequate teachers from the classroom.

To compound the problem, these laws also vary considerably from state to state. For this reason, it seems to us that the most feasible way to examine this national dilemma is in microcosm. As a good case in point, we offer South Carolina, a state in which teachers are protected from arbitrary discharge by a continuing contract system (established by the 1974 Employment and Dismissal Act). More important, South Carolina's system closely resembles the continuing contract and tenure systems of other states. Because of this resemblance, we believe the South Carolina example can be instructive for principals and boards elsewhere in the United States who are asking themselves, "What exactly does state law say about the discharge or decertification of a teacher? Why is the law structured the way it is? Does the law actually make discharge and decertification as difficult as people say? Are there ways we can make the current law work to promote educator competence?"

Evolution of a Law

Local school boards in this country have

---

*This article was co-authored with Suzanne H. McDaniel.

traditionally been granted in law the authority both to
hire and discharge teachers. By the same token, state
boards of education have been granted the authority by
state legislation both to certify and decertify teachers. These grants of authority, which were designed to
give local and state boards control over the quality
of teaching in the local districts and in the state,
were expressed in broad terms for many years. In the
1960s, however, a series of federal court cases based
on the Fourteenth Amendment pointed out the need to
modify these broad grants of authority by specifying
as much as possible the reasons for which a teacher
could be discharged or decertified and the procedures
local and state boards must follow before depriving a
teacher of a particular job or of a livelihood.

In 1966, federal courts settled three major South
Carolina cases dealing with the discharge of teachers:
Williams v. Sumter School District #2, Bradford v.
School District #20, and Rackley v. School District #5.
While the facts in the three cases differed, the major
principles established in the court rulings did not.
In all three cases, the courts upheld the right--actual-
ly, the "duty to the public"--of the local board to
supervise the conduct of teachers and to discharge
them, either by nonrenewal of contract or by dismissal
during a contract period, in proper cases. The phrase
"in proper cases" is a crucial one, since all three
decisions upheld the right of teachers to substantive
due process. The decisions emphasized that local
boards cannot use their authority to discharge teachers
in an arbitrary or discriminatory manner but must show
"good cause" for the dismissal. (Good cause, as the
courts saw it, does not include retaliation against a
teacher for exercising his or her rights as guaranteed
in the First Amendment.)

By affirming teachers' right to substantive due
process in discharge cases, the courts tacitly indicated
the need for some specific guidelines as to what constitutes "good cause." Some such guidelines were included in the 1974 South Carolina law regarding the
discharge of teachers.

Shortly after federal courts had established the
right of South Carolina teachers to substantive due
process, the U.S. Supreme Court, in deciding cases from
other parts of the United States, established the
principle, that, where a person can demonstrate the

20

existence of a property interest or a liberty interest
that is threatened by a government action, the person
is entitled to procedural due process before the
government can take action.

In Board of Regents v. Roth (1972), the Supreme
Court defined a liberty interest as existing when the
cause for nonrenewal of a teacher's contract could
damage the teacher's standing in the community and/or
when the negative inferences people might make from
the board's action could close the teacher off from
other professional opportunities. By inference, it is
clear that procedural due process would be necessary in
decertification cases, since denial of certification
involves a liberty interest; that is, it effectively
forecloses professional opportunities for the teacher
in the state and in other states having reciprocity
agreements with that state.

In Perry v. Sinderman (1972), the Supreme Court
defined a property interest to exist if the teacher is
tenured, if the teacher is dismissed during a contract
period, and/or if the teacher's contract is not renewed
even though there has been an implied promise of reemployment. (A continuing contract system like that
in South Carolina carries an implied promise of reemployment.)

Because of these cases, South Carolina educators
and legislators recognized the need for new legislation
that would specify both the causes for which teachers
could be discharged and the procedures local boards
must follow to dismiss a teacher or not renew a contract. In drafting this legislation, the committee
appears to have used a combination of tradition, 1962
South Carolina law, court decisions, and the experiences
of other states to draw up a list of "just causes" for
discharge. To establish procedural safeguards, the
committee seems to have relied partly on earlier provisions in South Carolina law, but primarily on guidelines for procedural due process established by the
United States Supreme Court in a welfare case,
Goldberg v. Kelly (1970). These guidelines required
that a citizen be guaranteed:

1. An opportunity to be heard "at a meaningful
time and in a meaningful manner"

2. A "timely and adequate notice" of the hearing

21

that details the reasons for the action being considered

3. The opportunity to confront and cross-examine witnesses

4. The opportunity to present oral and written evidence and arguments in his or her own defense

5. The right to retain an attorney

6. An objective determination of the case based solely on law and evidence brought out at the hearing

7. A written statement of the final decision and the reasons for it.

In 1974, the South Carolina legislature passed the Employment and Dismissal Act, which guaranteed substantive and procedural due process to teachers in discharge cases. In the same session, the legislature updated the law regarding decertification to guarantee similar "just cause" and procedures. These two sections of the 1974 code of school laws, although slightly modified in 1976, are essentially the same today.

The Current Law in South Carolina

Under the continuing contract system established by the 1974 law, an employed teacher is automatically guaranteed a contract renewal for the coming school year unless notified of nonrenewal in writing before 15 April. This clause implies a promise of reemployment and thus establishes a property interest for the teacher in his or her employment by the district. For this reason, the statute goes on to specify the exact procedures school administrators and local boards must follow if they wish to dismiss a teacher or not renew the teacher's contract.

As the Supreme Court of South Carolina has interpreted the law (Adams v. Clarendon County School District #2, 1978), discharge procedures can be initiated in two ways. If the cause for the discharge is "evident unfitness for teaching," the teacher must be given a written notice of discharge that states the reason or reasons for it and points out the teacher's right to request a hearing.

22

If, however, the cause for the discharge is "deficiencies or shortcomings other than those which manifest an evident unfitness for teaching but which do, nevertheless, constitute improper performance of employment duties," the teacher must be given preliminary notices, written by administrator--principal or supervisor--and calling the deficiencies to the teacher's attention, suggesting ways the teacher could improve, informing the teacher of evidence in his or her file, and pointing out the teacher's right to examine the file.

The principal or supervisor must follow up these notices by trying to help the teacher correct the problem and then allowing a reasonable time for the teacher to show improvement. (Six weeks has been considered a reasonable amount of time by some courts.) If the teacher does not show significant improvement, a formal written notice of discharge can be given to the teacher. (The law specifies that registered mail must be used to deliver formal notices.)

Once formal notification has been received, the teacher has fifteen days in which to request a hearing. If the teacher does not make such request, he or she is considered to have waived the right to be heard. If, however, the teacher does make a written request, the local board must set a date for the hearing within ten to fifteen days from receipt of the request. At least five days before the hearing date, the teacher must be notified in writing of the time and place set by the board. According to precedents in case law, the time and place selected by the board must demonstrate respect for the rights of the employee; that is, both time and place must be convenient for the employee, and the space chosen must be large enough to accommodate any witnesses the employee intends to bring.

The hearing must be public unless the teacher has filed a written request to the contrary. The teacher may attend the hearing and be represented by an attorney. (The board need not provide an attorney for the teacher, however. Most local teachers' organizations will provide counsel for their members.) The board is empowered to subpoena witnesses both for the schools and for the teacher, although it may limit the teacher's witnesses to ten. The subpoenas are to be served by the county sheriff and enforced by the Court of Common Pleas that has jurisdiction in the area.

All testimony at the hearing must be given under oath and recorded by a reliable recorder. The cost of the services of a professional court reporter is shared equally by the teacher and the board. During the hearing, the teacher may present "any and all defense," cross-examine witnesses, and show evidence in his or her own behalf.

Following the hearing, the board has ten days in which to render its decision. The decision is considered final unless, within thirty days, the teacher files an appeal with the Court of Common Pleas. Within thirty days of the appeal, the local board must file a certified transcript of the hearing record. The appeal is then conducted in accordance with civil court procedures in South Carolina, but the Court of Common Pleas and the South Carolina Supreme Court--if the appeal goes that far--may consider errors in law only. The findings of the local board are considered final with respect to fact. If the Court of Common Pleas or the State Supreme Court finds the local board in error, it can assign payment of damages and court costs. The amount of damages may not exceed two years' back pay reduced by amounts the teacher earned or could, with diligence, have earned during that time period. Damages for wrongful dismissal are usually assigned to the local board as agent for the school district; however, in some cases where maliciousness on the part of a principal or board member has been instrumental in the discharge, damages have been assigned to those individuals.

The procedures spelled out by the 1974 Employment and Dismissal Act are echoed in the 1974 law regarding procedures the State Board of Education must follow in decertification cases, with minor differences in timing. (State board members have to assemble from all parts of the state, necessitating more time for their actions than for the actions of a local board.)

Besides delineating procedural due process, the 1974 Employment and Dismissal Act lists grounds on which a local board may base the discharge of a teacher. Two major grounds are specified in the law; first, "failure or incompetence to teach as directed by the superintendent" and, second, "evident unfitness for teaching" as shown by any of the following: 1) persistent neglect of duty; 2) willful violation of rules and regulations of the district board; 3) drunkenness; 4)

24

violation of South Carolina or United States law; 5) gross immorality; 6) moral turpitude; 7) dishonesty; or 8) illegal use, sale, or possession of drugs or narcotics. The law clearly states that this list of causes is not exhaustive. That the courts will uphold other interpretations of unfitness than those mentioned specifically in the law was demonstrated in Adams v. Clarendon County School District #2. In that case the State Supreme Court ruled that a teacher's deficiencies in basic language skills showed him to be unfit to teach in an institution charged with the task of imparting those same skills to others.

Although "moral turpitude" is defined in the South Carolina criminal code, most of the supposedly specific "just causes" for discharge are expressed in such general, undefined terms that they pose problems for administrators and board members who must determine just what actions each "cause" includes. In interpreting the terminology, administrators and boards have had to look to case law, which provides some—but not enough—guidance. The term "incompetence to teach," for example, has been held by various courts to mean anything from failure to maintain discipline, to failure of a teacher's class to make normal progress, to the teacher's slothful appearance in the classroom. "Gross immorality," too, has been variously interpreted by the courts to include not only sexual activity that runs counter to community standards, but also non-sexual offenses against the prevailing code of morality. Even though courts have interpreted these and other broad terms differently, they have established certain questions that administrators and boards must be able to answer affirmatively before the causes for a discharge can be considered just:

1. Is there objective, well-documented evidence—not hearsay—to support the discharge?

2. Is a pattern of behavior established by the evidence?

3. Is more at issue than a personality clash or a philosophical conflict between a teacher and an administrator?

4. Is there a clearly documentable relationship between an objectionable act by the teacher and the teacher's effectiveness in the classroom or his or her

25

functioning as a part of the school community?

5. Are the quality of instruction and/or the status of the school system in the community detrimentally affected by the teacher's action(s)?

6. If a violation of rules and regulations is involved, were those rules or regulations clearly established (preferably in writing), generally understood, and compatible with the First Amendment as interpreted by the courts?

These same questions must be considered by the State Board of Education in analyzing whether there is just cause for decertification. There are only twelve grounds on which a teacher can be decertified: 1) incompetence; 2) willful neglect of duty; 3) willful violation of rules and regulations of the state board; 4) unprofessional conduct; 5) drunkenness; 6) cruelty; 7) crime against South Carolina or United States law; 8) immorality; 9) any conduct involving moral turpitude; 10) dishonesty; 11) evident unfitness for the position for which employed; or 12) sale or possession of narcotics.

These are the only causes that may be used as grounds for decertification. The list is an exhaustive one because decertification is a much more serious step than discharge. The causes listed are, however, basically the same as those for discharge, and they are expressed in the same general terms. Only "unprofessional conduct" is specifically defined in the law; one evidence of it is breach of contract. It is unclear whether there are other types of unprofessional conduct not stated by the law. In the absence of more specific definition of these terms, the state board, too, must rely on guidelines for substantive due process established in case law.

Implications for Principals and Boards

As the law stands, principals in any state who wish to recommend the discharge of incompetent or unfit teachers should keep substantial written files on all teachers who have obvious deficiencies or shortcomings. These files must include documentation of the deficiencies, evidence that help has been provided, and evidence of teacher improvement or lack thereof. The files must also include records of not just one observation and follow-up conference, but of several, so that a pattern of deficiency or incompetence is established.

This requirement means the principal must become a critic (in the most negative sense) rather than an instructional leader. It means the conscientious principal has to spend many hours observing in class-rooms, holding follow-up conferences, and providing teachers with whatever instructional assistance they need. But there are always other, equally pressing demands on a principal's time. When one of these competing demands has to give way, it's often the time spent documenting teacher deficiencies. Why? There are many reasons, but the most important ones may be these:

1. The requirements of the law cast the principal in the two conflicting roles of evaluator and consultant. Principals who have trouble reconciling or balancing these two roles (possibly the majority of them) often opt for the more positive role of consultant rather than the negative role of evaluator. Some principals may abrogate their responsibilities in this area entirely and busy themselves with their other duties.

2. Under any circumstances, discharging an employee is an action involving interpersonal conflict. That conflict is intensified when it is embodied in a formal hearing process, which establishes an adversarial relationship between principal and teacher. Many people understandably prefer to avoid such conflict if at all possible.

3. Deficiencies are often evident in a teacher's work during the first year of teaching, but principals generally tend to give beginning teachers the benefit of the doubt. After allowing deficiencies for a year, some find it difficult to change tack and reprimand teachers the second and succeeding years for something they got by with the first year. (This is one reason why South Carolina, like many other states, has established a probationary period for beginning teachers.)

4. The possibility of being assigned damages if the court finds any maliciousness or discrimination on the part of the principal may hold many back from

27

vigorous pursuit of their duty in discharging teachers. The persistent observation and record-keeping required by the law, some fear, could be interpreted as malicious harrassment by the teacher and, perhaps, even by the courts.

Clearly, the tasks facing the principal who recommends the discharge of a teacher can be time consuming and unpleasant, but if both principal and board are committed to ensuring competent instruction, the process prescribed in the law can be used to discharge the incompetent in such a way that the action will most likely be upheld by the courts. If the prescribed procedures seem too conflict laden, a district can make the task less onerous by dividing the responsibilities among administrators to lessen the evaluator-consultant role conflict. For example, curriculum consultants could take primary responsibility for assisting teachers in improving instruction, while the principal takes primary responsibility for evaluation. Where curriculum consultants are not available, perhaps an assistant principal can fill the consultant role. In any case, the principal, as the direct agent of the board and the superintendent in the school, should do the evaluating; and for that reason, in hiring principals, districts should take into account each applicant's strengths and weaknesses in the evaluation of teacher competence.

The lessons from the South Carolina story are many, and they are clearly significant for boards and administrators in other states as well. In general, those who are responsible for discharging and decertifying teachers--and that includes principals, supervisors, superintendents, and local and state boards of education--should take care to:

· Know the details of state law in terms of "just causes" for dismissing and decertifying teachers.

· Know the details of state law in terms of exact procedures to be followed in removing a teacher.

· Know precisely the "property" and "liberty" interests that may characterize a teacher's contract status.

· Make every effort to inform teachers (in writing) of deficiencies in their performance and help them

28

improve within a "reasonable" period of time.

·Know what constitutes adequate documentation, accepted as such by courts in the state.

·Keep carefully documented files (open to teachers for inspection) regarding teachers' deficiencies and administrators' efforts to promote improvement.

·Document a pattern of specific conduct and behavior that qualifies as "incompetence to teach," "evident unfitness for teaching," "immorality," "moral turpitude," "dishonesty," or "unprofessional conduct." (You must show that the behavior in question actually impairs teaching effectiveness.)

·Take advantage of any assistance that may be available from other district personnel in documenting a teacher's incompetence or unfitness to teach.

·Make sure that charges against a teacher are based neither on personality conflicts nor on constitutionally protected rights of the teacher.

·Give formal notice of discharge by registered mail, outlining at that time all due process rights of the teacher.

These are demanding procedures, but most state statutes and both state and federal case law (especially federal "due process" decisions) require such steps when tenured teachers are discharged.

Admittedly, while the law's due process provisions do safeguard teachers, they also tend to discourage some administrators and boards. Nevertheless, it is by no means impossible under the law to discharge or decertify a teacher, nor is the process required by law nearly so complicated as some administrators claim. (For some, the law may in fact provide a rationale for not doing what they do not want to do.) Because ensuring competent instruction sometimes requires the dismissal of an incompetent tenured teacher, administrators must be willing to comply with the legal guidelines for such decisions. A law is, after all, made effective by the people who enforce it.

THE NTE AND TEACHER CERTIFICATION

On April 12, 1977, a three-judge federal district
court panel handed down a ruling in U.S. v. State of
South Carolina upholding the authority of South
Carolina to employ the National Teacher Examination
(NTE) in certifying and determining pay scales of
public school teachers. Neither the Fourteenth Amendment nor Title VII of the Civil Rights Act, said the
judges, has been violated by South Carolina's past or
present policies. The court decided that the state of
South Carolina had not been motivated to discriminate
against minority groups (blacks, in particular) by its
adoption of the NTE for certification and salary purposes. Finally, the court ruled that the NTE "had some
rational relationship to . . . legitimate employment
objectives" and that the massive validation study conducted by the state and the Educational Testing Service
(ETS) was a satisfactory substantiation of current
score requirements for certification in different teaching fields. The court noted that the state had satisfied the "business necessity" requirement set out in
the landmark Griggs v. Duke Power Company decision
(1971). The background of the South Carolina case and
the implications of the decision warrant closer
inspection.

Historical Background

The NTE was first used in South Carolina as an
element in the certification of teachers in 1945.[1] Before that time, under the dual school system called
for by Article II of the South Carolina constitution,
there were two distinct and unequal salary schedules
for white and black teachers. In an apparent attempt to
remedy obvious discrimination, the State Department of
Education decided to establish a single but graded
salary schedule. From 1945 to 1969 all teaching certificates were given a grade (A, B, C, D) on the basis
of scores achieved by the teacher on the Common Examinations of the NTE, and the grade--along with such factors
as teaching experience and level of education--became a
determinant of salary paid to the teacher.

In 1969 the state adopted new regulations that required applicants to achieve a composite score of 975
on the NTE for a professional certificate--but graded
certificates per se were discontinued. Under the new

regulations a teacher holding a graded certificate could either keep it or convert it to a professional certificate by obtaining the required NTE score of 975. Many teachers, a high percentage of them blacks, have not made the required score.

On December 8, 1972, the president of the South Carolina Education Association advised the state superintendent of education that a suit would be filed unless the State Board of Education recommended to the legislature "that the present use of the National Teacher Examinations in South Carolina in regard to salary, tenure, or promotion be discontinued, effective July 1, 1973." After considerable study at the state department level, a subsequent board recommendation "to eliminate the effect of the NTE as a salary determinant by the beginning of the 1974-75 school year," and a plan to phase out salary differentials for holders of the old graded certificates, the state department found that the legislature's Budget and Control Board was apparently unwilling to appropriate the $2 million necessary to finance the first year of the three-year phase-out.

In September, 1975, the National Education Association (NEA), the South Carolina Education Association (SCEA), and nine black teachers joined the U.S. Department of Justice in a class action suit against South Carolina and all the state's school districts, charging that use of the NTE discriminates against blacks and therefore violates the equal protection clause of the Fourteenth Amendment and Title VII of the Civil Rights Act of 1964.[2] It should be noted here that the Equal Employment Opportunity Act of 1972 amended Title VII to include public employees.[3] Consequently, the Justice Department has been particularly interested in the disproportionate impact on minority applicants for teacher certification that could result from the fixed NTE score requirement.

In this morass of conflicts and issues--which has included teachers, the NEA, the SCEA, the State Department of Education, the State Board of Education, the legislature, and the Justice Department--there has been another party to the debate: the Educational Testing Service. Carrying on something of an up-and-down relationship with the South Carolina Department of Education over the years, ETS in 1973 informed State Superintendent Cyril Busbee that "if . . . NTE scores continue

to determine salaries of experienced teachers in South
Carolina, beginning May 1, 1974, ETS no longer will report NTE scores to the South Carolina Department of
Education." This deadline was extended to August 31,
1975, to give the General Assembly further opportunity
to eliminate the graded certificates.

On another front, however, ETS joined with the
State Department of Education to conduct a validation
study of the NTE in an attempt to head off a legal
decision that would, as it did in a 1975 North Carolina
case,[4] question the arbitrariness of the required NTE
score. Under the agreement, ETS rescinded its
ultimatum, in part on the condition that the cut-off
score of 975 be subjected to a validation study. In
the fall of 1975 centers were established in Charleston,
Greenville, and Columbia; and 456 college faculty
members representing the 25 state-approved teacher
training programs participated on 26 panels during the
three-month study to validate NTE scores. In the summer
of 1976 a new set of validated NTE scores, a direct result of the study, was announced, to become effective
in the certification of teachers after November 1,
1976. Rather than a single score, each teaching area
would require a different level of performance on the
NTE, ranging from a low of 940 for agriculture teachers
to a high of 1,178 for media specialists.

Between the summer of 1976 and April of 1977 the
state department—and, indeed, all the defendants and
plaintiffs—awaited the decision of the court on the
several legal issues involved. Professional Certificates and one-year Temporary Professional Certificates
(the only teaching licenses now issued in South
Carolina) were granted to those who qualified after
November 1 by attaining the newly validated NTE scores.

Legal Issues and Determinations

The court first examined the constitutional issues
raised by this case. The plaintiffs had charged that
the NTE discriminates against blacks as a class, since
historically blacks have, on the average, performed
less well on this test than have whites.

Citing the U.S. Supreme Court's decision in
Washington v. Davis, the court held that it was necessary for the plaintiffs "to prove that the state
intended to create and use a racial classification."

33

Following an extensive review of historical events in certification changes in South Carolina and a statistical analysis of the impact of the NTE score requirements on blacks seeking certification, the court asserted, "We are unable to find any discriminatory intent from these facts." The court viewed the increasingly higher scores required between 1945 and 1976 not as a means of discrimination but as the state's effort "to redefine minimal competence from time to time [that] cannot reasonably be questioned."

On this fundamental issue relating to the Fourteenth Amendment, the court concluded:

> . . . [T]he plaintiffs have not demonstrated the required discriminatory intent with respect to any of the specific decisions setting certification standards based on NTE scores. This is especially true in connection with the state's 1976 change in requirements where there is no indication whatsoever that the state and its officers were motivated by anything more than a desire to use an accepted and racially neutral standardized test. . . .

Pointing out that the plaintiffs had not established that the NTE itself discriminates on the basis of race and that the content validity of the test creates classifications on a permissible basis (knowledge and skill), the court ruled that the state did not violate the Fourteenth Amendment by using this test in making certification decisions. That differentiated pay schedules--based in part on NTE scores--were in effect is not significant, since the court was "unable to find an intent to discriminate."

This did not end the inquiry, however. The NTE, as employed in South Carolina, had also been challenged under Title VII of the Civil Rights Act of 1964. Thus the court examined whether use of the NTE in certification met the "rational relationship" and "business necessity" concepts established by earlier court cases under Title VII. In Washington v. Davis the U.S. Supreme Court had determined as follows:

Under Title VII, Congress provided

34

that when hiring and promotion
practices disqualifying substantially disproportionate numbers
of blacks are challenged, discriminatory purpose need not be
proved, and that it is an insufficient response to demonstrate
some rational basis for the challenged practices. It is necessary,
in addition, that they be "validated"
in terms of job performance . . .
perhaps by ascertaining the minimum
skill, ability, or potential necessary for the position. . . .

Since the plaintiffs had demonstrated that the
NTE scores disqualified a substantially disproportionate
number of blacks, the burden of proof shifted to the
defendants to show that the test was 1) rationally
related to job performance, 2) properly validated,
and 3) a business necessity.

It should be noted that there was already a bench-
mark case by which South Carolina could measure its
actions in this case. The August, 1975, federal district court decision U.S. v. State of North Carolina
made it clear--while striking down an arbitrary score
of 950 on the NTE for certification--that "the state
of North Carolina has the right to adopt academic
requirements and written achievement tests designed and
validated to disclose the minimum amount of knowledge
necessary to effective teaching." Indeed, the court
all but encouraged North Carolina to reinstate the
NTE once a score or scores were validated, since, as
the ruling stated, "nothing contained herein shall
be deemed to prevent the state from reinstating a written test cut-off score provided that such cut-off
score shall first have been validated with respect to
minimum academic knowledge." It was with this precedent
in mind that South Carolina, in cooperation with ETS,
undertook its validation study in the fall of 1975.
In general, both ETS and the courts have supported the
validated use of scores for initial certification.

In the present case in South Carolina, the court
ruled that "the design of the validation study is
adequate for Title VII purposes." Robert M. Guion, a
nationally recognized tests and measurement authority,
testified that in his opinion the validation study met

35

all the requirements of the American Psychological Association Standards as well as guidelines set by the Equal Employment Opportunity Commission (EEOC). With the support of other testing experts and a decision by South Carolina state department officials to establish scores somewhat lower than those validated "to account for various statistical and human factors," the court affirmed the new validated scores in effect after November 1, 1976. Since these validated scores are higher than previous scores required for certification, the issue of past requirements was dismissed. It was noted by the court that only for agriculture (940) was there a lower validated score than the prevailing score of 975 in effect from 1969 to 1976.

Last, the court considered the "business necessity" test requirement set out in Griggs. Even though South Carolina does not intentionally discriminate against blacks as a class by using the NTE and uses a properly validated test that is rationally related to job performance, the court still had to determine whether or not there was an alternative practice that would achieve the "business purpose" equally well but with a lesser disparate impact by race. The plaintiffs suggested one alternative here--graduation from an approved program of teacher education. The court, however, said, "We cannot find that this alternative will achieve the state's purpose in certifying minimally competent persons equally as well as the use of a content-validated standardized test. . . . These scores for certification purposes survive the business necessity test under Title VII." In like manner, the court held, pay distinctions based on NTE scores also pass the "rational relationship" and "business necessity" tests.

Educational Implications

The federal panel in the South Carolina case came down clearly on the side of the state. Every argument advanced by the attorney general and plaintiff-intervenors (including the National Education Association) was rejected. The use of validated NTE scores both for certification purposes and salary purposes was for the first time, unequivocally affirmed. Perhaps because the plaintiffs could provide no satisfactory alternative, the court held that the "business necessity" test had been met. However, even though the validation study itself was ruled appropriate and the

36

NTE was judged rationally related to the performance of the teacher, some problems and questions remain.

First, there is no question but that this decision--if it is not reversed--will in fact affect blacks more than whites. How <u>much</u> it may affect them is undetermined at this point. A North Carolina official has estimated that about 30% of the blacks who have taken the NTE there have failed to score 950, whereas only 2% of the whites who have taken it have failed. What percentage of blacks in South Carolina will be eliminated by the even higher scores validated by the ETS study? What effect will this <u>actually</u> have on the teaching force and on teacher education, especially for blacks? This is an important social and educational question for the immediate future.

Secondly, how much of a rational relationship <u>actually</u> exists between a test of cognitive knowledge and teaching performance? Although the court was satisfied that South Carolina had met the court requirements, a nagging question persists: Why do some people who do poorly on the NTE turn out to be, in the judgment of supervisors, good or excellent teachers? Why do some people who score quite well on the NTE turn out to be ineffective teachers? It is no doubt true, as a federal court said in a similar case in Mississippi (1972), that a written test (like the NTE) "measures only a fraction" of teaching ability or potential. Cognitive knowledge of one's subject and of professional education is an aspect of professional competence--but how <u>much</u> of a determinant of teaching effectiveness is this in relation to such qualities as personality, commitment, flexibility, sense of humor, and hard work?

Third, even though the validation study conducted by the state and ETS met the court requirement for a validated test, how much reliance can <u>actually</u> be placed on the study? In spite of impeccable psychometrics, the validation study conducted in the fall of 1975 depended heavily upon the "professional judgment"-- or the subjective opinion--of the panels of teacher educators. Content review panels were asked to make "judgments of whether or not the content of each question in the test is covered by the teacher education program" and also "judgments of the relation between the description of the test content . . . and the curriculum in terms of omissions or overemphasis."[5] Knowledge estimation panels took on the even more subjective task of providing "estimates of the percentages of minimally knowledgeable candidates who would be expected to know the answers to individual test questions."[6] The concept of "minimally knowledgeable candidates" was to be determined by each member of the panel, and then an estimate of how many such individuals (in terms of a percentage) would be able to answer questions was to be made. I myself participated on one of these panels and found the process a highly subjective one, to say the least. Although the judgments to be made were professional, the task of guessing how many "minimally qualified" individuals could answer a given question must raise some questions about the objectivity--and validity--of the study, even though the court was satisfied.

Educators in America should take a close look at the South Carolina controversy and the court case that has resulted from it. Whether their interests center on legal issues, certification standards, teacher education, tests and measurements, educational policy, or sociology and philosophy of education--they will find significant implications for their profession. No doubt many will applaud the decision as an important step, in this era of teacher surplus, toward limiting the number of certificates issued by a state and toward producing a more exclusive cadre of professional teachers. Others, no doubt, will focus on unresolved problems and implications of the decision. But for the moment, at least, the court has established important guidelines legitimating the use of validated NTE scores in the certification of teachers.

FOOTNOTES

1. Some of the information for this historical sketch is contained in an unsigned, informal paper prepared by the State Department of Education titled "The Use of the NTE for Salary Purposes for Experienced Teachers." The court decision, a 45-page ruling, included extensive historical notes.
2. Betty E. Sinowitz, "Teachers Fight Misuse of National Teacher Exams," Today's Education, January/ February, 1976, p. 108.
3. Paul L. Tractenberg, "Legal Issues in the Testing of School Personnel," Phi Delta Kappan, May, 1976, p. 603.
4. United States v. State of North Carolina, 400 F.

Supp. 343 (E.D.N.C. 1975), _vacated_, 425 F. Supp.
789 (E.D.N.C. 1977).
5. Memorandum to panel members from the state superintendent, Fall, 1975.
6. _Ibid_.

SOUTH CAROLINA'S EDUCATOR IMPROVEMENT ACT:

PORTENT OF THE SUPER SCHOOL BOARD?

South Carolina is not often considered to be in the forefront of educational change. But the state has adopted an Educator Improvement Act that Josef Stulac, director of the task force established by the new state law, calls "the most comprehensive and ambitious education law in the country today."

"Other states are looking at our legislation as a possible model," Stulac says. "How well we implement the Educator Improvement Act may determine how quickly other states follow our lead."[1]

What makes this law--initially designed to take effect in 1981-82--so important? What does it augur for public education in South Carolina and the nation?

Act 187, the Educator Improvement Act, passed by the South Carolina General Assembly and signed into law in August 1979 by Gov. Richard Riley, is designed "to provide for the training, employment, and evaluation of public educators." Its specific goals are to upgrade standards for educators, to insure that prospective teachers have basic skills (reading, mathematics, and writing), to improve educator training programs, to insure that prospective teachers know and understand their teaching areas and are helped to achieve their teaching potential, and to develop evaluation instruments and standards by which to judge classroom teachers as professional practitioners. More specific provisions of the law mandate a complex and comprehensive system of screening and testing from the prospective teacher's freshman or sophomore year of college to initial certification, provisional contracts, and (eventually) continuing contract status.

The new law also established the Educator Improvement Task Force--with its own director, staff, and governing board (made up of legislators and educators)-- as the state agency charged with implementing the new act. The task force is responsible for developing basic skills tests and subject-area examinations for teachers-in-training and observation instruments to be used in evaluating preservice and inservice teachers.

This "cradle-to-grave" system of training, certification, employment and evaluation is more than a testing bill, however; its provisions touch all facets of
the education enterprise. The outline below, prepared
by the task force, shows the intricate pathway to a continuing contract that the Educator Improvement Act
establishes. Note that all steps in the process provide
for feedback and assistance to teachers in relation to
strengths and weaknesses identified by evaluation
instruments:

Prospective teacher education students (freshmen
and sophomores):

1. pass a basic skills examination in reading,
   writing, and mathematics before being admitted
   to a teacher education program;
2. receive results of the examination from the
   state department of education and the commission on higher education in a form that provides specific information about strengths and
   weaknesses;
3. receive counseling from the state department
   of education and the commission on higher
   education to help improve performance;
4. may take the exam no more than three times;
   and
5. may receive conditional admission, not to exceed one year, to a teacher education program.

Student teachers (juniors and seniors):

1. complete one full semester of student teaching;
2. are observed at least three times by trained
   observers who are representatives of the college or university; and
3. receive assistance, training, and counseling
   from the college or university to overcome
   identified deficiencies.

Prospective teachers (juniors and seniors):

1. complete academic requirements for teaching
   from an approved college or university; and
2. pass a teaching area examination and receive
   the results from the state board of education
   in a form that provides specific information
   about strengths and weaknesses.

42

Colleges and universities:

1. receive results of the basic skills examination from the state department of education and the commission on higher education;
2. receive results of the teaching area examinations in a form that will assist them in identifying strengths and weaknesses of their teacher training programs;
3. receive advice and aid concerning curricula and standards by which programs are approved; and
4. participate in program review by visiting teams trained in program approval procedures.

Provisional contract teachers (first year):

1. are observed at least three times by trained observers who are representatives of the school district;
2. receive from the school district written evaluations that provide information concerning strengths and weaknesses;
3. receive from the school district advice and assistance to remedy detected deficiencies;
4. participate in staff development programs focused on identified deficiencies; and
5. may be employed in another district under a new one-year provisional contract, if the current evaluation is unfavorable.

Annual contract teachers:

1. are observed at least twice by representatives of the school district;
2. receive results of the evaluation from the school district;
3. receive counsel from the school district concerning strengths and weaknesses;
4. participate in staff development programs offered through the school district to offset deficiencies; and
5. may be employed on annual contracts for a maximum of four years.

Continuing contract teachers (whose duties include classroom teaching):

1. are observed periodically by representatives of the school district;
2. receive counsel concerning strengths and weaknesses from the school district;
3. participate in individual or group staff development programs offered by the school district to offset identified deficiencies; and
4. must earn credits for recertification in courses relevant to the area of recertification.

It is not surprising that there is now a flurry of activity in South Carolina. Countless open forums and meetings disseminate progress reports and secure input, but a good bit of confusion and consternation persists among affected constituencies. The South Carolina Association of Colleges for Teacher Education (SCACTE) has raised questions about funding, testing, and student teaching. Who will pay for the administration of basic skills tests and for remediation of identified weaknesses? Will private colleges receive funds for remedial programs? How often (and where) will basic skills tests be given? How long is a semester of student teaching, and must it be full time? Can all colleges modify their calendars to accommodate a full semester of student teaching? Who is a "public educator"? Principals, vice principals, supervisors, school psychologists, guidance counselors, and librarians are not now included, according to the state attorney general.

Public school personnel also have concerns. Who will observe all these teachers, and who will train the observers in the use of the new instrument?[2] (In the fall of 1980 a survey of more than 19,000 South Carolina educators asked who should perform observations. Responses ranked in this order: 1) principal, 2) master teacher in the area, 3) peer teacher, 4) curriculum specialist, 5) self-report of the teacher being observed. Pilot projects to train observers in the use of the Assessments of Performance in Teaching instrument are being conducted now.) Can we really create effective staff development programs on the basis of identified weaknesses? Who will pay for these programs?

Finally, there are persistent legal, educational, and philosophical questions about the use of tests in evaluating teaching. Can the state legally require students in a private college to pass a basic skills

44

test as an entrance requirement for their major program? What levels of validity and reliability must be met by the basic skills test, the teaching area examinations, and the evaluation instrument? Will rigorous testing programs create improvement: or only fear, conformity, and red tape? Can one instrument assess "teaching performance" for all subject areas and grade levels?

The new law calls for continued use of the National Teacher Examination (NTE), long a controversial policy in South Carolina.[3] In teaching areas where no validated NTE tests exist, the law requires the state to develop its own tests. Unfortunately, the NTE area examinations are norm referenced rather than criterion referenced, a fact that makes their use in identifying specific strengths and weaknesses of individuals or teacher education programs difficult. SCACTE has recommended substituting criterion-referenced area examinations, but this would require a change in the law and the constructing of more than 65 new area tests. The task force agreed that new criterion-referenced tests would be more useful. However, the attorney general has now ruled that new tests can be developed only for the 10 teaching areas for which no validated NTE area exams exist. Using different types of tests for similar purposes may pose thorny legal problems for the state in the event of an "equal protection" suit.

In response to this plethora of issues and questions, the legislature has granted a one-year delay in implementing the law to allow for resolution of logistical problems and for development and validation of tests. This extension gives colleges another year to adjust calendars for the full semester of student teaching--now determined to be a minimum of 60 teaching days. It also gives school systems time to gear up for the classroom observations and staff development requirements. Needless to say, the additional time is particularly necessary for the development, field testing, and validation of the Education Entrance Examination (EEE), the Teacher Area Examinations, and the Assessments of Performance in Teaching (APT) observation instrument. Testing and funding are the greatest concerns of educators during this period of transition.

A Chinese maxim warns us that "it is difficult to prophesy--especially in regard to the future." Nevertheless, the Educator Improvement Act has implications for public education nationwide. I believe the major implication of this act is its contribution to the evolving concept of the super school board at the state level.

Most educators know that the U.S. Constitution gives states "plenary power" over educational policy under the 10th Amendment. The Constitution itself makes no mention of education, and so education has become one of those powers not assigned to the federal government nor denied to the states. Historically, states have provided through their state constitutions such offices and agencies as the state superintendent, the state board of education, and the state department of education. But they have assigned policy making and the day-to-day operation of public schools to local boards of education. Such "grassroots" boards have been charged--both by tradition and by state law--with governing local schools in such vital areas as funding, teacher employment and dismissal, curriculum, and supervision of instruction. The last decade, however, has witnessed the demise of local board autonomy and the rise of another, more powerful school board--the state legislature itself.

One of the major forces behind the new super school board has been the increasing federal role in education over the last half century, both through Congress and the courts. Congress has used its power of taxation to raise and expend public funds for education to meet various "general welfare" and "national defense" needs in U.S. society. Typically, federal aid to education has been targeted at such problems as agriculture (e.g., the Smith-Hughes Act, 1917), vocational training (e.g., the Civilian Vocational Rehabilitation Act, 1920), space-race technology (e.g., the National Defense Education Act, 1958), poverty (e.g., the Elementary and Secondary Education Act, 1965), and special education (e.g., the Education for All Handicapped Children Act, 1975). Federal aid to education is typically funneled through state governments, a practice that magnifies responsibility for education at the state level. For example, in the Education for All Handicapped Children Act, state departments of education are required to monitor local education agencies to insure compliance with the regulations of P.L. 94-142. The role of the states in making education policy is likely to be even stronger when the new Reagan "block grant" system for allocating federal funds goes into effect.

Even more than Congress, the federal judiciary has influenced the creation of the new super school board. Much has been said about the power of the federal courts to limit the jurisdiction of state government. But the more important consequence of court decisions in such areas as segregation, financing, and teacher/student rights has been to limit the policy-making and decision-rendering powers of district and county boards of education. Federal courts have said, in effect, that education is a state responsibility and that the state must insure that delegating the management of education to local boards does not result in grossly unequal funding, dismissal of teachers or expulsion of students without due process, or discriminatory districting practices. Recent court decisions remind state legislatures that they, not local boards, exercise plenary power over education.

A second force that has contributed to the rise of the new super school board has been the increasingly activist posture of state legislatures. Responding to a perceived "will of the people," legislatures have taken action in such areas as basic skills instruction, minimum competency levels for high school graduation, and measures of teacher accountability. Public concerns about fiscal responsibility and academic literacy have encouraged state legislators to intervene in educational policy heretofore left primarily to local boards. Whether political "expediency" or "statesmanship" is the motivating power, state legislators believe that testing teacher and student competence may be the remedy to widespread voter concern over the quality of education. Legislatures appear to be saying that local boards of education and colleges that prepare teachers have not measured up to societal expectations. Consequently, the competence of students and teachers will be judged by state-mandated tests.

The most significant implication of South Carolina's Educator Improvement Act may be that the state legislature has established clearly its intention to use its plenary power over education. South Carolina has already passed a Serrano-type finance act (1977) and a basic skills act (1978). Now this new piece of comprehensive legislation completes the picture--a picture whose outlines may well trace an image of the future in other states. We may expect legislatures in other states soon to exercise major decision-making

power in the field of education, particularly over the
education and employment of teachers. Whether such
policy making at the state level improves the quality
of teaching and learning remains to be seen.

FOOTNOTES

1. In a presentation to the South Carolina Association
    of Colleges for Teacher Education (SCACTE) at the
    31 October 1980 meeting in Columbia, South Carolina.
2. The law charges the Educator Improvement Task Force
    with developing and validating the observation/
    evaluation instrument.
3. Thomas R. McDaniel, "The NTE and Teacher Certifica-
    tion," Phi Delta Kappan, November 1977, pp. 186-88.

TEACHING SPECIAL CREATION AND EVOLUTION IN THE
PUBLIC SCHOOL: THE LEGAL QUESTIONS AND QUANDARIES

> Who can say that evolutionary
> philosophy is not significant
> when it has been made the
> basis of social Darwinism,
> economic and military
> imperialism, anarchistic
> individualism, fascism, com-
> munism . . ., racism, modern-
> ism, atheism and practically
> every other harmful philosophy
> known to man?
>   Henry M. Morris

The question I would like to pursue in this article
is a legal, educational, political, and religious one:
What is the proper role of the public school in teaching
evolution and/or special creation as scientific truth?
Perhaps nowhere else in contemporary American society
is the intersection of controversial and conflicting
perspectives on evolution more manifest than in the
public school, and, consequently, this question has had
a long and interesting history. The basic question
above has many variant forms: Should the school teach
evolution as fact? As theory? Can a state legally ban
this subject matter from the curriculum of public
schools? Is evolution part of a "secular religion"?
If evolution as an explanation of the origins of man
conflicts with the religious beliefs of students, should
they be exempt from compulsory biology classes in which
evolution is taught? Does, then, required instruction
in evolution violate freedom of religion? Is it
Constitutional to teach the Genesis account of creation
instead of evolution? As a balance or alternative to
evolution? If scientists develop scientific evidence
in support of the Genesis account of "divine" or
"special" creation, can such scientific theory/evidence
be legislated by state governments to be included in
science curriculums? The public school has been a
crucible in which public policy about the nature and
import of evolution has been forged. The questions
debated--by educators, politicians, scientists, and
religionists--have created both quagmires and quandaries
but few clear resolutions.

49

One of the best ways of tracking the debate is by way of legislation and court battles. Courts exist to resolve conflict in accordance with the principles of law. In our court system those principles of law are found in precedents established by case law, and, ultimately, in the broad principles outlined in Federal and State Constitutions. Whenever the issue of teaching evolution has become a matter for the courts to decide, the legal principle of religious freedom has been at the heart of the debate. That principle (made binding on state legislatures by the Fourteenth Amendment) is found in the Federal Constitution's First Amendment, which says: "Congress shall make no law respecting the establishment of religion nor prohibiting the free exercise thereof." The two parts of this amendment have been called the "establishment clause" and the "free exercise clause"; each clause has been important in the legal debate concerning the teaching of evolution in public schools. In general, Supreme Court (and lower court) decisions have upheld principles of "neutrality" and "separation of church and state." The First Amendment, as one judge put it, "does not tolerate laws that cast a pall of orthodoxy over the classroom." With this brief background in mind, let us examine several important court cases dealing with the teaching of evolution.

The well-known Scopes "monkey trial" of 1925 revolved around concepts of religious and academic freedom and, more specifically, considered whether or not Scopes, a high school biology teacher, was in violation of the Tennessee statute prohibiting the teaching of "any theory that denies the story of the Divine Creation of man as taught in the Bible, . . . instead that man has descended from a lower order of animals."[1] More famous than John Scopes--who came from and quickly returned to obscurity--were fundamentalist prosecution lawyer William Jennings Bryan (a former Presidential candidate) and agnostic defense lawyer Clarence Darrow (the foremost criminal lawyer of the time). The judge in this case refused to consider the validity of the Darwinism theory of evolution, saying that the only question was whether or not Scopes had in fact taught the theory of evolution.

Although Darrow devastated Bryan in a culminating cross-examination that showed Bryan to be less than expert in his knowledge of both Scripture and science, Scopes was convicted and fined $100. In an appeal to the Tennessee Supreme Court that decision was unanimously overturned--on the technical grounds that only a jury could fine someone more than $50. The Tennessee Supreme Court did rule that the statute was Constitutional but because the decision against Scopes himself was reversed, an appeal by Scopes to the U.S. Supreme Court was precluded. However, the net effect of the Scopes trial was to slow down the fundamentalist drive to enact similar "anti-evolution" statutes in other states. In fact, only two other states--Mississippi and Arkansas--succeeded in passing such laws in the late 1920's.

It was not until 1968 that the First Amendment Constitutional question in the anti-evolution statutes of state legislatures was faced head-on by the U.S. Supreme Court. In the case of Epperson v. Arkansas, the Court dealt with the Arkansas statute that had been modelled on the Tennessee law at issue in the Scopes trial. The administration of a high school in Little Rock, on the recommendation of biology teachers in the system, adopted and prescribed for the 1965-66 school year a text containing a chapter on "the theory about the origin . . . of man from a lower form of animal."

Susan Epperson, a tenth grade biology teacher at Central High School, faced an interesting dilemma. Should she defy the state law and teach the chapter (a criminal offense), or should she refuse to follow the directive of school authorities and violate her responsibilities to the superintendent and board of education? She went to court to resolve her dilemma, asking for a declaration that the state law is void and enjoining the school system from discharging her for teaching evolution. The Chancery Court held the statute to be unconstitutional, a violation of the First Amendment because it, "tends to hinder the quest for knowledge, restrict the freedom to learn, and restrain the freedom to teach."[2] Thus, this lower court held the anti-evolution law to be a violation of Epperson's academic freedom. However, the Supreme Court of Arkansas reversed the Chancery Court on the grounds that this statute was simply a curious but altogether proper exercise of a state government's power to determine the public school curriculum.

The U.S. Supreme Court sided with Epperson and overturned the Arkansas Supreme Court. Justice Fortas in the majority opinion said:

51

The overriding fact is that Arkansas
Law selects from a body of knowledge
a particular segment which it proscribes
for the sole reason that it is deemed
to conflict with a particular religious
doctrine; that is, with a particular
interpretation of the Book of Genesis by
a particular religious group. . . .
Government in our democracy, state and
national, must be neutral in matters
of religious theory, doctrine, and
practice. It may not be hostile to any
religion or to the advocacy of no
religion; and it may not aid, foster,
or promote one religion or religious
theory against another. . . . This
prohibition is absolute. It forbids
alike the preference of a religious
doctrine or the prohibition of theory
which is deemed antagonistic to a
particular dogma. . . . In the present case, there can be no doubt that
Arkansas has sought to prevent its
teachers from discussing the theory
of evolution because it is contrary to
the belief of some that the Book of
Genesis must be the exclusive source
of doctrine as to the origin of
men. . . . Arkansas' Law cannot be de-
fended as an act of religious neutrality.

In this important decision the Court declared unconstitutional those laws which prohibit the teaching of
evolution in public schools.

An altogether different tack was taken in the early
1960's, initially in California but soon after in many
other states, as concerned citizens attempted to exercise some control over the teaching of evolution in
science classrooms. With some assistance from the
State Superintendent of Education Max Rafferty, some
California parents convinced the State Board of Education to establish a policy that would require teachers
and texts to describe evolution as only a theory or
hypothesis--not scientific truth. Indeed, it is
apparent that publishers of science texts in the 1980's
are treating evolution in a more cautious manner than
ever before. As a 1981 Holt, Rinehart & Winston text
Living Things says, "Darwin asked some interesting

52

questions and set forth a thought-provoking hypothesis about which people are seeking new clues in the light of modern science."[3]

But even more significantly, the California protest against evolution--strongly backed by the San Diego-based Institute for Creation Research--has led to the introduction of "equal treatment" bills in a number of states. Between 1964 and 1978 twenty-two bills and in 1979 and 1980 eleven bills were introduced to require that "creation science" be given equal time in _science_ classes.[4] The momentum of this movement was slowed somewhat when a 1973 "Genesis Law" was ruled unconstitutional by the Sixth Circuit of Appeals. The Court, persuaded by the arguments of the National Association of Biology Teachers, called this law a new version of "the legislative effort to suppress the theory of evolution which produced the famous Scopes Monkey Trial of 1925."[5] Scientific Creationism, roundly attacked by most scientists, is currently the focal point of debate about the teaching of evolution in public schools.

Creation science is promoted primarily by a small group of religious fundamentalists holding membership in the Creation Research Society (CRS). They subscribe to a basic tenet that Genesis presents a _scientifically_ verifiable account of origins and have developed related research hypotheses capable, they insist, of evolution by scientific procedures. They also attack evolution as a "mere theory," a secular dogma, and a humanistic religion. Specific positions developed by creation scientists (primarily at the Creation Science Research Center in San Diego) include the following:

1) Biological life began only five to six thousand years ago[6]

2) Creation of the natural world occurred in a single creative act over the span of a week

3) God designed permanent basic forms; nature is static and predictable

4) Christianity is necessarily opposed to evolution

5) Evolution is not substantiated by fossil evidence; all fossils were actually deposited at the time

of Noah's Flood

6) Evolution violates the second law of thermo-
dynamics (which says that entropy increases in a closed
system)

7) There are no genetic connections between major
groups of life forms

8) All known change in non-living material is
degenerative, from complex to simple elements; therefore, in living organisms all mutations are deleterious

9) Evolution is a "belief" or "dogma" and support
of its teaching by a law establishing curriculum is an
act of "indoctrination"[7]

10) All questions of origins are beyond the reach
of science as the scientific method can only be applied
to the present, observable world.

The last point is a particularly interesting one since
it appears to exclude creationism, as well as evolution,
as a scientific endeavor. Nonetheless, the elements of
the creationists' position can be seen in two recent
court cases, the first in California.

In the 1981 case of Segraves et al v. State of
California, the plaintiffs--citing their belief in
scientific creationism--brought suit against the California State Board of Education for its "Science Frame-
work for Public Schools." Seagraves contended that
these guidelines promulgated the theory of evolution
as the only credible theory of life, a theory which
conflicted with personal religious beliefs of the
Seagraves family. Thus, the teaching of evolution is
indoctrination and coercion violating First Amendment
"free exercise" of religion rights of the three
Seagraves children. Moreover, the teaching of evolution
was held to establish a religion of secular humanism,
thus violating the establishment clause of the First
Amendment.[8] The case avoided the hard issues--those relating to the scientific validity of evolution and
creationism--and focused instead on the issue of
religious freedom. In Just of 1981 the court ruled
that the state board had in no way acted to deny the
Seagraves children free exercise of religion. This
ruling seriously undermines the creationists' contention
that evolution is a religion.

The state legislatures of Arkansas and Louisiana each voted in 1981 to approve a "Balanced Treatment for Creation Science and Evolution Science Act." In a highly publicized case early in 1982, <u>McLean v. State</u>, U.S. District Judge William Overton struck down Arkansas' law, declaring that it was "simply and purely an effort to introduce the biblical version of creation into the public schools."[9] He concluded that this act's real effect was the advancement of the religious doctrines of the creationists and that was "an excessive and prohibited entanglement with religion." As an interesting note, Judge Overton observed that the draft of the prototype of the bill at issue had been written by a South Carolina fundamentalist Christian who was a respiratory therapist "trained in neither law nor science" and who believed evolution to be the forerunner of such wrongs as racism, Nazism, and abortion. The judge concluded his decision by saying, "no group, no matter how large or small, may use the organs of government, of which the public schools are the most conspicuous and influential, to force its religious beliefs on others."

After a half-century of legal debate, certain principles seem at this point to be well established:

·Evolution as an aspect of science cannot be excluded by law from the curriculum of public schools.

·Government must remain neutral in matters of religion and may not aid, foster, or promote religious beliefs.

·Evolution is not religion but science and as such when prescribed in science courses does not violate a student's "free exercise" of religion.

·Creation science is primarily a religious belief and as such has no legal standing as science in a public school curriculum.

·Equal treatment laws establish a particular religious belief and as such entangle the state in the promotion of religion.

But other court cases (perhaps one day a Supreme Court decision) may provide new directions to and new principles for this controversial issue, one not likely to disappear soon.

The legal question is only one aspect of this controversy, of course. Other questions that confound and prolong the discussion include such intractable inquiries as these: How scientifically (and literally) should Genesis be understood? Is the science class-room--where ideas must be considered at least potential-ly falsifiable--a proper place to study an idea revered as holy?[10] Are the biblical account of origins and the theory of evolution competing alternatives? Does suppressing scientific creationism square com-pletely with principles of academic freedom? Is creation science forever bound to be part of a religious system? Does the fact that creationism re-quires a supernatural explanation automatically exclude it from the realm of science? Is evolution necessarily atheistic? (William Mayes declares that "evolutionary theory is no more atheistic than atomic theory, the germ theory of disease, or the kinetic theory of gases."[11]) Just how "testable" are the evolution theory and the creation-science model? If a court decided to let "equal treatment" prevail, what effect would this have on the concept of state "neutrality"? Does teaching evolution (or creation science, for that matter) constitute "indoctrination"? Who should decide what is science and what is religion?

Such questions, naturally, are both intriguing and endless. Perhaps in the continuing debate about the proper role of the public school in teaching evolution, answers to these and other questions will be found. Be-cause Americans take seriously their religious beliefs, the explanatory power of science, and the influence of public education on the values of the young, that debate is an important one indeed.

FOOTNOTES

1. As cited by Jerry R. Tompkins (ed.) in D-Days at Dayton: Reflections on the Scopes Trial (Baton Rouge: Louisiana State University Press, 1965), p. 3.
2. As quoted by David Fellman (ed.) in The Supreme Court and Education, third edition (New York: Teachers College Press, 1976), p. 114.
3. As quoted by Henry P. Zuidema, "Less Evolution, More Creationism in Textbooks," Educational Leader-ship, vol. 39, no. 3, December, 1981, p. 217.

4. Gerald Skoog, "Legal Issues Involved in Evolution vs. Creationism," _Educational Leadership_, vol. 38, no. 2, November, 1980, p. 154.

5. Jerry P. Lightner, "Tennessee 'Genesis Law' Ruled Unconstitutional," _NABT News and Views_, vol. 10, no. 2, April, 1975, p. 5.

6. Dorothy Nelkin, "Science, Rationality and the Creation/Evolution Dispute," _Social Education_, vol. 46, no. 3, April, 1982, p. 264. For other detailed analyses of creation science and its basic propositions see also Preston Cloud, "Scientific Creationism--A New Inquisition Brewing?" _The Humanist_, vol. 37, no. 1, January/February, 1977. Also see Richard D. Alexander, "Evolution, Creation, and Biology Teaching," _The American Biology Teacher_, vol. 40, no. 2, February, 1978. For an analysis from the creationist perspective see Henry Morris _et al._, _Science and Creation_ (San Diego: Creation Science Research Center, 1971). Several of these characterizations of scientific creationism and evolution are included in the South Carolina Balanced Treatment for Scientific Creationism and Evolution Act of 1981, a prototype bill now being considered by several legislatures.

7. Harvey Siegel, "Creation, Evolution, and Education: The California Fiasco," _Phi Delta Kappan_, vol. 63, no. 2, October, 1981, p. 96. This is a particularly searching analysis and criticism of creation science.

8. Thomas J. Flygare, "The Case of _Seagraves v. State of California_," _Phi Delta Kappan_, vol. 63, no. 2, October, 1981, p. 98.

9. "Newsnotes," _Phi Delta Kappan_, vol. 63, no. 7, March, 1982, p. 499.

10. Alexander, _op cit_, p. 91.

THE PRINCIPAL'S SCHOOL LAW QUIZ

Few principals are as well versed in matters of school law as they need to be. That is understandable, of course, given the complexity of statutes, the constant flux of case law, and the vague or conflicting decisions of courts. To keep the principal up-to-date, I have designed a true-false checklist to assess his or her grasp of important school law guidelines governing such topics as teacher and student rights, punishment, negligence, and defamation of character. There are a few half-truths here and a few of my "right answers" can be debated; however, I think the underlying principles and reasoning in my explanations will be helpful to the school administrator. Do not look at the answers until you try your own hand at the quiz!

_____ 1. Expulsion of a handicapped student from school requires more due process procedures than for other students.

_____ 2. A teacher's right to free expression away from school is the same as any other citizen's right.

_____ 3. Teacher's beards, mustaches, hair length is regarded as symbolic free speech, but schools can require these to be "well-groomed."

_____ 4. Schools may not regulate teacher dress.

_____ 5. If a student is permanently injured by corporal punishment, the court may not hold a teacher negligent if the student's behavior warranted stern disciplinary action.

_____ 6. If corporal punishment is administered to the same degree for every student who is so punished, the courts would probably uphold the teacher in a suit against him for that very reason.

_____ 7. Teachers may be liable for gossip they spread about students in the teacher's lounge, even if they are not misrepresenting the truth.

_____ 8. A student's locker is his property while it is assigned to him and, therefore, cannot be

59

searched without a warrant.

_____ 9. A teacher has no responsibility for what happens to a student off school grounds and/or in non-school activities (e.g., at home).

_____ 10. If a parent signs a permission slip for her child to go on a field trip, the teacher bears no legal responsibilities for injuries or accidents to that child during the trip.

_____ 11. A teacher is responsible for warning children of potential dangers involving experiments, class activities, and faulty physical conditions in his or her classroom.

_____ 12. If an injury occurs in a teacher's class while he or she is absent, the teacher is always liable for the damage.

_____ 13. Teachers generally have little to fear in the way of libel suits if they communicate their knowledge or evaluation of a student in good faith to a person who has a right to the information.

_____ 14. Teachers are not generally liable for unforeseeable accidents that happen to their students during a class.

_____ 15. Teachers supervising playgrounds, lunch rooms, study halls, or bus duty have no legal responsibility for pupil injuries in these situations.

_____ 16. Under the doctrine of in loco parentis a teacher has the same rights to discipline a child as the parent does.

_____ 17. If in a private conference with a teacher the principal suggests that the teacher is "incompetent" (even though the principal has no evidence of incompetency), the teacher could probably win a defamation of character suit.

_____ 18. A teacher's comments on permanent record cards can be grounds for a libel suit.

_____19. A teacher can photocopy a "reasonable" number of workbook pages for students who need extra help in the classroom.

_____20. The Bible can be taught as literature or history in a public school.

Answers

__T__ 1. The 14th Amendment provides "due process," the courts have decided, for students who are expelled (or even short term suspensions of 3-5 days) as well as for teachers who are discharged. Under P.L. 94-142, the Education For All Handicapped Children Act, special due process requirements are established to ensure the handicapped 1) the right to an "appropriate education," 2) the right to remain in the student's present placement until the resolution of any complaint, 3) the right to an education in the "least restrictive" environment, 4) the right to have all changes of placement made in accordance with the prescribed procedures. Courts (e.g., Stuart v. Nappi 1978 Connecticut) have been ruling that such provisions for the handicapped take precedence over local/state procedures for expulsion. A recent Indiana case (Doe v. Koger) held that a child can't be expelled if his handicap is the cause of his misbehavior. These procedures and rulings may be weakened under the Reagan administration.

__T__ 2. Actually, a half-truth. Court cases have established full citizenship rights for teachers--but the sensitive nature of a teacher's responsibility for nurturing the young requires consideration, in holding employment in a school, of the effect of one's actions on morale in the school, reputation, and instructional success.

__T__ 3. Another half-truth. This battle was apparently won in the federal courts in the 1960's under 1st Amendment protection of freedom of speech. Teachers' beards are, the courts reason, a part of the individual. There has been no Supreme Court case in this area of the law, however, and more conservative trends in the 1980's could influence federal courts to be more restrictive. In 1978, for example, the Fifth Circuit Court of Appeals held that the dismissal of a nontenured teacher for refusing to shave his beard did not impair his constitutional rights since shaving did not attach to him "a badge of infamy." Unwritten rules in this area are considered arbitrary and insufficient cause for dismissal, however. A 1978 Florida case upheld a dress code forbidding _student_ mustaches.

F 4. The difference between beards and dress is that dress may be changed at will after a teacher is "off duty." Courts tend to support dress codes for teachers as a reasonable condition of employment (and not an infringement of their personal liberty). Dress codes for students are generally upheld when based on consideration of health, safety, and "decency." Of course, "decency" can be a tricky concept since this depends to a degree on the eye of the beholder. A key factor is whether the particular "indecency" can be shown to be "distractive" or "disruptive" to the educational process.

F 5. Permanent injury can never be justified as "reasonable." This is probably the most damaging evidence against a teacher in a negligence or assault and battery case.

F 6. Corporal punishment, case law has determined, should be individualized. The teacher must take into account such individual differences as age, health, size, previous misbehavior, the nature of the offense, etc.

T 7. Teachers have "qualified privileged communication"--which means that so long as they communicate 1) in good faith 2) information they believe to be correct 3) to a person who has a right to that information (e.g., a guidance counselor or a prospective employer), they are not defaming character by slander or libel. Gossip in a faculty lounge probably does not fall under a teacher's protection. Teachers should report knowledge about criminal acts they learn of from students. If

a student admits to using drugs, a teacher
may (but doesn't have to) communicate this to
the parents as they are generally included
within the "confidential relationship."

F   8. Lockers are school property and may be
searched at the administration's pleasure.
School authorities generally may "search"
when they have "reasonable suspicion" and
are not held to the higher standard of
"probable cause" for police search. Most
(but not all) courts have held that school
officials are not acting as state officials
when conducting "warrantless searches" of
individual students and therefore are not
violating 4th Amendment protection. Higher
standards are being required in recent cases,
however. In 1979 the Second Circuit Court
of Appeals affirmed the lower court decision
that while "reasonable suspicion" of a crime
could justify searches of a student's pockets
and outer garments, strip searches of
students must be based on "probable cause."
In 1980 the Seventh Circuit Court of Appeals
ruled in the 1980 Doe v. Renfrow case that
"dog alerts" established cause for searching
outer garments but not a strip search.

F   9. This is often true but exceptions exist. For
example, P.L. 92-247 requires teachers to report any suspected cases of child abuse. In
one interesting case a shop teacher was held
liable when a youngster who made a toy cannon
in class, took it home, loaded it up with
"cap powder" and bee-bees, and shot his
brother's eye out. The court say the teacher
should have warned students against such
"foreseeable dangers." This "foreseeability"
concept is basic to most negligence cases.

F 10. While it is always a good idea to require
permission slips--because this shows good
planning and gives parents both advanced information and an opportunity to object to a
particular trip--permission slips do not
absolve teachers of their duty to supervise
and to provide in loco parentis protection
from harm. A parent cannot sign away his
children's right to such care. Teachers

63

should plan trips carefully, develop and teach safety rules, secure licensed drivers, and have an adequate number of supervisors.

T 11. To minimize occasion for negligence suits a teacher should always try to anticipate potential dangers for children and eliminate hazards. Courts ask, "should a 'reasonably prudent' teacher have foreseen the danger?" Certainly, teachers should warn children to be careful when any possible harm to them might be in the offing.

F 12. The teacher may be liable but is not always so. A court will employ "foreseeability" and "reasonable prudence" questions in deter-mining liability: Why is the teacher absent? Would he have been able to prevent the accident if present? What kind of class did he leave and how mature were the students? Did the teacher instruct the class in how to behave in his absence? What other arrange-ments (student monitor, message to the teacher next door) were made? Did injury occur because the teacher was absent or because of student misconduct (which might be "contributory negligence")? Younger students may be presumed incapable of contributory negligence.

T 13. See question #7. The key to defamation of character torts (civil wrongs) is intention. Defamation involves 1) a false statement about a person which is published or communi-cated; 2) the statement brings hatred, dis-grace, ridicule, or contempt to the person; 3) damages result from the statement. Is the teacher trying to damage a student? Or is he merely communicating, in his official capacity as teacher, information to someone (parent, college admissions counselor, employer) who has a right to the information?

T 14. Again, the important question is would a reasonably prudent teacher have anticipated the accident and prevented it by a) elimina-ting risky activities or physical hazards b) warning children of potential dangers? In recent years--as teachers have secured professional status--the standard of care has been raised from the reasonably prudent <u>person</u> norm on the presumption that teachers ought to have more prudence than the average person. Still, teachers are not expected to be clairvoyant nor to prevent "acts of God."

__F__ 15. Teachers have the same liability for negligence in supervising such activities as in classrooms. One teacher was held liable for an accident on the playground while she was supervising by watching through the window from inside her classroom. The most important protection for a teacher is to <u>be</u> where assigned to be.

__F__ 16. Parents have much more latitude in disciplining their children (everything short of child abuse) than do teachers. When a teacher's punishment is arbitrary, capricious, or excessive--or motivated by spite, malice, or revenge--the teacher may be held liable for negligence or (even) assault and battery. If a child becomes violent or physically abusive, a teacher may employ that physical force necessary to restrain the student, but must not become the aggressor.

__F__ 17. If a principal is informing a teacher of an evaluation, the communication is presumably "official," rather than a personal attack on a teacher. (See reasoning in answers to questions 7 and 13.) The principal's intention would appear in this case to be to communicate in good faith a job-related judgment that the teacher has good reason to receive. That the conversation is <u>private</u> indicates that the principal is not intending to bring ridicule to the teacher and has not communicated the evaluation to a third party outside the privileged communication. On the other hand, if a teacher is dismissed for what he or she says in a private conversation with a principal that teacher may have court ordered reinstatement. In one case (<u>Givhan</u>, 1979), a teacher was reinstated after being fired following such a conversation in which she had made "petty and unreasonable demands" in an "insulting, loud, and hostile" manner.

The Supreme Court held that her right to freedom of speech had been violated by the principal and the board.

T 18. Particularly in light of the "Buckley Amendment" (the Family Educational Rights and Privacy Act of 1974), teachers should take care not to libel students with unwarranted and inaccurate assessments of their character. Comments such as "ruined by whiskey and tobacco," "this boy would be all right if it weren't for his father," and "this girl is tricky and unreliable . . . and destitute of womanly virtues" have resulted in damages being awarded to students. Teachers should strive to be descriptive, objective, positive, and accurate when writing about students.

F 19. Guidelines under the new copyright law are quite strict. Photocopying has become so commonplace, however, that teachers violate provisions of law daily. Some teacher texts explicitly permit unrestricted copying and some even provide pages for masters--but most workbooks and texts retain copyright protection.

T 20. Several Supreme Court cases (e.g., Schempp and Murray, 1963) have clearly prohibited religious worship in public schools, since freedom of religion may be denied to non-Christian (even non-religious) students who are compelled by governmental laws to attend school. The Supreme Court has noted that whether or not religious observances in schools are voluntary is irrelevant. Courts have invalidated observance of holy days, display of religious symbols, religious clubs (which cannot meet on public school premises during lunch or after school unless renting space). "Silent meditation" periods are generally upheld by courts. The Eighth Circuit Court of Appeals in 1980 affirmed a South Dakota decision permitting the singing of Christmas carols in school assemblies. A recent Supreme Court per curiam ruling (1980) rejected a Kentucky law requiring the Ten Commandments to be posted in classrooms. As with other decisions in this area of law, the Court determined that this law was advocating an obvious religious preference and that the Ten Commandments themselves were more religious in nature than historical-cultural (especially the first three).

If you scored 15 or more "correct" responses, your basic understanding of school law principles is satisfactory or better. On the other hand, if you had difficulty with the quiz and/or found the explanations foreign, you might consider a brush-up course or some additional reading in this area of your professional knowledge.* One thing is certain: in our litigious age every principal must stay well informed in matters of school law.

---

*See, for example, M. Chester Nolte, How to Survive in Teaching: The Legal Dimension (Chicago: Teach 'Em, 1978); Louis Fischer, David Schimmel, and Cynthia Kelly, Teachers and the Law (New York: Longman, 1981); and Martha McCarthy and Nelda Cambron, Public School Law: Teachers' and Students' Rights (Boston: Allyn and Bacon, 1981). See also Thomas R. McDaniel, "The Teacher's Ten Commandments," Phi Delta Kappan, June 1979; "Corporal Punishment and Teacher Liability: Questions Teachers Ask," Clearing House, September 1980; and (with Suzanne McDaniel) "How to Weed Out Incompetent Teachers Without Getting Hauled into Court," National Elementary Principal, March 1980.

CORPORAL PUNISHMENT AND TEACHER LIABILITY:

QUESTIONS TEACHERS ASK

Introduction

Since we live now in an age of litigation, teachers need to be aware of their legal liabilities and to avoid actions which may result in a court case. Pupil punishment is an increasingly important area of legal concern for educators. Teachers have a responsibility to protect students in their care from injury, to act as a "reasonably prudent" teacher would act to prevent loss or damage to their students, and to exercise judicious "in loco parentis" authority over students to correct misbehavior and provide for their orderly instruction. Whenever a teacher is the responsible <u>cause</u> for pupil injury--so often the case when punishment is involved-- the possibilities of a negligence suit are great.

But if this is an age of litigation it is also an age of school violence, crime, and disruption.[1] The Supreme Court has upheld the use of corporal punishment to discipline students (<u>Ingraham v. Wright</u>, 1977). Now 40 states authorize corporal punishment by law with only New Jersey and Massachusetts having laws prohibiting its use.[2] With our contemporary back-to-basics approach that stresses more law-and-order in the classroom, teachers are often expected by school boards and administrations to exercise greater control over misbehaving students. Such an expectation is likely to increase instances of punishment (corporal and noncorporal) of students and, consequently, instances of negligence cases brought against teachers. Finding alternatives to legally dangerous punishment practices is a high priority for educators.

The classroom teacher, caught between conflicting forces, will need to develop greater understanding of both the legal liabilities of improper punishment and the effective means of establishing good discipline in the classroom. Let us examine a few of the central questions--legal and pedagogical--that exist or are emerging in the area of pupil punishment and suggest some general responses to those questions.

Questions About Pupil Punishment

What is corporal punishment? This is a form of corrective discipline that involves physical force and the inflicting of bodily pain on the student. Typically, corporal punishment practices include paddling (with or without an instrument), slapping, cracking hands with a ruler, pinching, pushing, hitting, hammerlocks and other wrestling holds, and exotic techniques such as finger holds ("milk the rat") and ear twists. In some cases courts have extended the definition to include threatening gestures and psychologically damaging techniques of punishment that humiliate students or create mental anguish.

Does a teacher have as much authority to punish as the parent? No. Although the legal authority to punish a child is granted to the teacher under the doctrine of in loco parentis, a teacher is not the parent and in the eyes of the court has less authority.[3] As student rights and the professional status of teachers have grown in recent years, the doctrine of in loco parentis has waned. Parents are liable for child abuse, of course, but otherwise have great latitude in punishment; teachers must justify punishment and defend themselves against negligence charges when punishment is arbitrary, capricious, or "excessive." Teachers may have to prove they acted prudently and fairly in administering "moderate" punishment for corrective purposes. Parents increasingly view teachers as highly trained personnel in the helping professions who should be accountable for delivering contractural services. Courts are also expecting a higher standard of prudence and professional expertise from teachers in negligence cases.

What evidence is most damaging to a teacher charged with excessive corporal punishment? Probably permanent injury to the student. Courts will not consider as "reasonable" or "moderate" punishment which disfigures or disables a child. In cases of mental anguish the court may rely on expert witnesses such as psychiatrists to establish the injury that is the basis of this negligence suit. Although corporal punishment is not by definition "cruel and unusual punishment," permanent injury may so qualify. If the injury resulted from aggravated attack on the student, assault and battery charges may also be brought against the teacher.

In corporal punishment situations is due process required? In 1975 the Supreme Court had affirmed a lower court ruling (<u>Baker v. Owen</u>) setting up procedural guidelines for corporal punishment. This decision required teachers to 1) inform students of offenses that might result in paddling; 2) punish only in the presence of a witness; and 3) provide the parent upon request a written explanation of the reasons. The Ingraham Case in 1977 overturned such provisions, declaring that "the Due Process Clause does not require notice and a hearing prior to the imposition of corporal punishment in the public schools. . . ." However, following procedures like those outlined in <u>Baker</u> is still a good idea, and some states have specific requirements legislated.

<u>If a teacher administers corporal punishment in anger, does a court consider that fact?</u> Oh, yes. Courts always consider all of the circumstances surrounding corporal punishment when a teacher is charged with negligence or assault and battery. Teachers have a professional relationship to students, are mature and prudent adults, and are to use corporal punishment only to serve an "important educational interest" (<u>Ingraham v. Wright</u>). Therefore, any evidence that a teacher has been rash or intemperate--motivated by spite, malice, or revenge--is quite detrimental to the teacher's defense. Using physical force to restrain a student from harming himself or others is justifiable unless excessive.[4]

<u>If a teacher consistently administers corporal punishment to the same degree for all offenders, does this help protect him?</u> No. To the contrary, common law principles suggest that it is incumbent upon a teacher to take into account the age, sex, and physical condition of each child when administering corporal punishment. That sex is to be a factor is interesting since Title IX requires <u>equal</u> treatment of boys and girls. "Physical Condition" may involve size, health, and strength of the student. In short, punishment--like instruction--should be individualized.

<u>What if a teacher does not know about the special health problems of a child?</u> This issue is less than clear in the law. The Baker case followed a traditional line of cases holding that if a student is supersensitive physically or emotionally to corporal punishment, the parents or the student must so declare ahead of punishment for a future case to be decided for the student on these grounds. Other precedents put greater responsibility on the <u>educator</u> to find out what special

71

health problems exist. At least in some jurisdictions
a teacher who, for example, strikes a hemophiliac or a
child with brittle bones may be liable for resultant
damages, even when the teacher is unaware of the
health problem.

Does it matter where corporal punishment is
administered on a child or with what instrument? Yes.
Since courts take all facts into consideration, they
will look at both of these questions. For example, one
teacher lost a suit when he struck a student on the ear
breaking an eardrum. The judge noted, "nature has
provided a part of the anatomy for chastisement and
tradition holds that such chastisement should there
be applied."[5] Teachers have lost cases for using
fists, belts, boards with holes and other instruments
deemed inappropriate for corrective punishment by the
courts.

Can a court decide that a teacher should not have
paddled a student in the first place? Certainly. One
of the issues a court considers is "substantive due
process." This issue revolves around the essential
question of fairness. Did the student break a rule?
What was the offense? Did it merit this particular
action by the teacher? Did the teacher try less
severe measures first? Was the student a problem case
who repeatedly failed to obey the rule in question?
Since the court must decide most cases on the "reasonably prudent person" criterion, the nature of the
offense is quite important in determining the reason-
ableness of the punishment.

What if parents tell teachers ahead of time not to
use corporal punishment? This is another gray area in
the law. At least one court, in a decision later overturned by the Supreme Court, (Glaser v. Marietta, 1972)
ruled that a parent's wishes in this matter must be
respected. The Supreme Court's Baker case suggested
that parents should notify the school of emotional
or physical health problems that could restrict the use
of corporal punishment. A rule of reason is that
schools should abide by a specific request from a
parent not to use corporal punishment. To disregard
such a request is to invite litigation.

Does corporal punishment work? Well, it may relieve some of a teacher's frustration, and it does seem
that some students have an almost masochistic need to

72

be punished to satisfy a perverted "attention need."
But most research says that corporal punishment at best
provides a temporary cessation of the punished behavior;
at worst it creates hostility and a desire for revenge
while teaching students that physical violence is a
legitimate way to solve problems. The American
Orthopsychiatric Association has come out against the
practice[6] as has the American Psychological Association,
the latter group contending that "physical violence
imprinted at an early age and the modeling of violent
behavior by punishing adults induces habitual violence
in children."[7] The National Education Association and
the American Civil Liberties Union[8] also have official
positions opposing corporal punishment for legal and
pedagogical reasons. Little scientific evidence
exists to support the practice.

Why, then, is corporal punishment so widely used
in schools today? There are a number of possible reasons for the continuing practice: tradition, immediate
results in many cases, occasional long-term success
stories, release of anger and frustration for teachers
and administrators, expressed desire by parents and
community leaders to continue the practice, community
concern for the lack of respect for authority among
students, teachers who are untrained in discipline
techniques, and a general belief that alternatives
either do not exist or do not work. Corporal punishment is often a "natural" response; it is inexpensive,
quick, and relatively simple to execute.[9] Many
teachers--despite official positions by professional
groups and a paucity of supportive evidence--honestly
believe corporal punishment to be a necessary support
for the authority of the teacher and an effective
measure in some cases.

What alternatives should schools and teachers be
acquainted with? Such approaches include behavior
modification (and token economies), Teacher Effectiveness Training, values clarification, moral education,
law-related education, suspension and in-school suspension, group counseling, parent involvement and parent
education projects, school-within-a school experiments,
student courts and negotiation processes, student codes
of rights and responsibilities, conflict resolution
programs, after-school behavior clinics, referral
programs, "commitment" contracts, assertive training,
transactional analysis, humanistic curriculum modification (e.g., Arthur Combs's), and self-concept

development strategies (e.g., William Glasser's and William Purkey's).[10] The NEA has developed alternatives to punishment through its Task Force on Corporal Punishment; the National Center for the Study of Corporal Punishment and Alternatives in the Schools is actively pursuing research; and the National Institute of Education has some related research projects on safe schools and student misbehavior.

Conclusion

Pupil punishment is an increasingly important dimension of a teacher's professional life and, especially in the case of corporal punishment, an aspect of teaching that can create legal difficulties for educators. Teachers and administrators can reduce the likelihood of liability by:

1) using corporal punishment sparingly and only for "good" reason;

2) warning students of offenses that may result in corporal punishment;

3) avoiding "excessive" punishment that might lead to physical or psychological injury;

4) employing "moderate" punishment to an "appropriate" part of the anatomy (not the head or spine) with an "appropriate" instrument;

5) following exactly state laws and school district policies governing punishment;

6) paddling only in the presence of a witness;

7) notifying parents of reasons for punishment if they request it;

8) respecting requests of parents not to use corporal punishment;

9) administering punishment in a calm manner, free of spite, malice, or revenge;

10) finding out (and communicating to student teachers and substitute teachers) any special health problems affecting punishment practices;

11) individualizing punishment to fit the nature of the offense and the age, sex, and physical condition of the child;

12) considering all consequences possible, especially if handicapped,[11] frail, or psychologically fragile children are to be punished;

13) carrying adequate liability insurance; and

14) staying abreast of legal developments in this area of school law.[12]

Given the range of punishment mishaps that could result in a negligence or assault and battery case--and given the weak pedagogical and psychological support for the effectiveness of corporal punishment--the best advice for teachers is to learn about and use a combination of alternatives to corporal punishment. These alternatives may require inservice training, extensive reading, cooperation among teachers (and support services and the community), curriculum revision, and patient dedication. For legal and educational reasons alternatives to punishment must be pursued--to keep teachers out of court and in effectively managed and well-disciplined classrooms.

NOTES

1. The Gallup Poll, as reported in the September, 1979 Phi Delta Kappan indicates that school discipline is perceived by the public to be education's greatest problem.
2. Tobyann Boonin, "The Benighted Status of U.S. School Corporal Punishment Practices," Phi Delta Kappan, January, 1979, p. 395.
3. Richard P. Hammes, "Tort and the Teacher: Some Considerations," The Clearing House, October, 1979, p. 107.
4. In the important recent case of Hall v. Tawney (1980), the Fourth Circuit Court of Appeals ruled on an issue of substantive due process, declaring that if corporal punishment "amounted to a brutal and inhumane abuse of official power literally shocking to the conscience" the court can assess damages against educators.
5. For this and other cases relating to teacher torts see my "The Teacher's Ten Commandments: School Law

in the Classroom," Phi Delta Kappan, June, 1979, pp. 703-708.

6. Myron Brenton, "A Further Look at Corporal Punishment," Today's Education, November/December, 1978, p. 53.

7. As quoted by Robert J. Trotter in "This is Going to Hurt You More Than It Hurts Me," Science News, November 18, 1972, p. 332.

8. For the ACLU's comprehensive position see Alan Reitman et al., Corporal Punishment in the Public School (New York: American Civil Liberties Union, 1972).

9. Brenton, p. 54.

10. For an examination of some of these alternatives and some bibliographic sources see my "Exploring Alternatives to Punishment: The Keys to Effective Discipline," Phi Delta Kappan, March, 1980. See also Eugene R. Howard, School Discipline Desk Book (West Nyack, New York: Parker Publishing Company, 1978); and Richard L. Curwin and Allen N. Mender, The Discipline Book: A Complete Guide to School and Classroom Management (Reston, Virginia: Reston Publishing Company, 1980).

11. For an interesting treatment of this issue see J. David Smith et al., "Corporal Punishment and Its Implications for Exceptional Children," Exceptional Children, January, 1979, pp. 264-268.

12. There are several good books and articles written to advise teachers of their legal liabilities. See, for example, Daniel L. Duke et al., "Emerging Legal Issues Related to Classroom Management," Phi Delta Kappan, December, 1978, pp. 305-309; Chester Nolte, How to Survive In Teaching: The Legal Dimension (Chicago: Teach 'Em, Inc., 1978); Rennard Strickland et al., Avoiding Teacher Malpractice (New York: Hawthorne Books, 1976); David Schimmel, Louis Fischer, and Cynthia Kelly, Teachers and the Law (New York: Longman, 1981).

PART II

ESSAYS ON SCHOOL DISCIPLINE

POWER IN THE CLASSROOM

One of the major issues in education today is "the discipline problem." Statistics on school crime, vandalism, and violence are astounding.[1] The public puts such emphasis on good school discipline that its absence is cited as the number one problem in American education today.[2] Classroom control is a major concern of most teachers too, and a spate of manuals and texts has appeared in the last decade to tell teachers how to survive, cope, and maintain sanity in the classroom.[3] More teachers lose their jobs for inability to manage classrooms than for any other single reason. The stress that is generated by tension between teachers and students has created a syndrome that has been accorded its own label now--"teacher burnout."[4]

In the face of the school's discipline dilemma, the response of school boards and educators has been to crack down on offenders, beef-up police measures in schools, reinstitute corporal and other forms of punishment, and back-up disciplining teachers with strong administrative support. The assumption seems to be that problems of classroom discipline can best be solved by giving teachers and administrators more power over student behavior. Will a return to the traditional, punishment-oriented, and authoritarian approach to discipline solve the discipline problem in American schools? Does punishment work? Will giving more control over student behavior to teachers, administrators, and school boards improve education? These are loaded questions, of course, since the terms solve, work, and improve have varying definitions. I want to examine the discipline dilemma, and selected approaches to it in the classroom, from an analytical point of view in an attempt to evaluate some assumptions about the ends and means of education as they relate to this particular issue. At the heart of my analysis of school discipline is the concept of power.[5]

The Authoritarian Approach

One approach to school discipline, briefly outlined above, is advocated by a large number of educators and citizens. Those who call for quick and stern retribution for deviant behavior, violation of rules, and lack of obedience to established social norms

employ an approach that is basically authoritarian in
nature. Authoritarians share a general set of attitudes and beliefs about education and discipline:

- •Power resides in the institution of the school as
  a mandatory mechanism of control and is assigned
  to authority figures, such as the superintendent,
  principal, and teacher. Students are assigned
  very little (if any) power.

- •Relationships of all kinds are viewed as hierarchical power structures and well-defined roles.
  (Research says that authoritarian personalities
  often gravitate toward the ministry, the military,
  government, and teaching--all of which have
  sophisticated hierarchies of roles.)[6]

- •Obedience and respect for authority are among the
  most important values that children must be
  taught.

- •Punishment is the manifestation of the authoritarian's power over underlings and is a necessary
  tool for sanctioning behavior and teaching respect for authority.

- •Because power is vested in the office or authority
  figure and behavior is rule-governed, student
  "misbehavior" is assumed to be a power play and
  thus a threat to the social order itself.

- •Students are "given" freedom only to the extent
  that they consent to conform to the standards of
  behavior required by the sources of authority;
  i.e., freedom is the granted liberty to act
  "correctly" in accordance with the social rules,
  norms, and expectations of authorities in power.

When a teacher views education as an authoritarian,
that teacher has a particular sensitivity to his or her
own power over students. Crow and Bonney draw this un-
lovely portrait of such a teacher:

> ...The authoritarian often views the
> classroom and his position in it as
> a source of almost unlimited power.
> He may view students as objects to
> be manipulated, used, or bullied....

78

> He probably has little patience with
> the concept of allowing students to
> voice an opinion different from his
> own....He places an inordinately high
> value on order, routine, and disci-
> pline. He may, for example, have
> numerous minor rules which tend to
> become as important as course content.[7]

The authoritarian teacher is always asking himself (and others) such questions as "How can I make these students behave? What punishments are most effective? How can I control my class if my principal doesn't back me up?" Authoritarians are convinced that the discipline problem can best be solved by restoring the traditional authority to the role of teacher, thus recreating respect and obedience in students.

The authoritarian approach to classroom discipline, then, is designed to increase a teacher's power over the actions of students. Strategies usually include some combination of the following principles and practices:

(1) Rules should be clearly and firmly established by the teacher. The teacher should attempt to identify a wide variety of unacceptable behaviors and prohibit these in his or her rules for students. From a practical standpoint, rules should be short, concise, and specific. They should be taught to students so that there is no misunderstanding about the rule itself or about the penalties for those who break the rules.

(2) Punishments should be swiftly and consistently applied when rules are broken. Tradition has supplied a host of punishments for teachers to employ: reprimands, deprivation of privileges, isolation (in the corner or the principal's office), extra homework, and paddling--to mention but a few. Punishments serve not only as consequences to broken rules, but as reminders of the power of a teacher to create unpleasantness for students. As Dobson says, "When a youngster tries...stiff-necked rebellion, you had better take it out of him. Pain is a marvelous purifier."[8]

(3) As the authority figure, the teacher is the judge of misbehavior. Teachers, therefore, must have good "command presence," be ready to make quick and

accurate judgments, and be alert to potential devi-
ates. Things happen in a classroom only with the
teacher's approval.

(4) A teacher's power may be enhanced by assertiveness training techniques. Frederick Jones suggests
the following approach to a resisting student:

> As soon as something starts, deal
> with it....Being assertive is the
> key....It's one thing to say "I
> mean business" and another thing
> to enforce it....Put your palms flat
> down on his desk and face him at his
> level. Stay there until he caves
> in.[9]

Other methods from assertiveness training--such as the
"broken record" technique--are also helpful in establishing teacher authority. Here the teacher keeps
repeating his or her request (no matter what a student
says to divert the teacher) so that the student learns
that the request is serious and that the teacher will
indeed persist until compliance is achieved.

Authoritarians, then, see power as a force vested
in roles of authority figures to be used to coerce,
command, and control the behavior of powerless students. It is manifested in directions, rules, and demands; student failure to comply results in punishment.
If punishments do not work, the teacher generally re-
fers the problem to a more powerful authority--such as
the principal or eventually the board of education itself. Each level of authority in the hierarchy has
more power than the one below it to employ punishment
and sanction. For example, a teacher may send the of-
fending student from the room; the principal may send
the student home for the day; the board may expel the
student from the educational system. Thus, power is
used to enforce rules and norms in the quest for
orderly and acceptable student behavior.

The authoritarian approach to school discipline
depends on the institutional and personal power of the
teacher. Its virtues lie in its simplicity, its long
tradition, its widespread public support, its ideal of
a harmonious social order where values of "respect" and
"efficiency" prevail. In many ways, the virtues of the

authoritarian school mirror the historical-cultural values of a constitutional republic--where initiation into the "power structure" of the society requires acceptance of the rules of the social order as a prerequisite to full participation. Without agreed-upon rules, roles, and standards both the republic and the school are in danger of anarchy and lawlessness.

On the other hand, a society which thrives on centralized authority where power resides only at the top of the hierarchical social structure can serve as the prototype of a police state. It may seem ironic that it is in a society where there is a puppet government that has no real power, where there is censorship of the press, where attendance at "cultural assemblies" is mandatory, and where anyone who tries to escape is tracked down and returned to the society-- in sort, in the American public schools--that we claim to be teaching democratic values. An excess of power in the offices of the society, and that "miniature society" (to use John Dewey's phrase) we call the school, is dangerous for democracy.

Furthermore, we know that punishment is not very effective in changing behavior. Although this staple of the authoritarian approach to discipline is well-ensconced in public school practice, its effects seem to be more negative than positive. The American Psychological Association claims that "physical violence imprinted at an early age and the modeling of violent behavior by punishing adults induces habitual violence in children."[10] At best, punishment strategies only temporarily suppress a behavior. If we know that punishment is ineffective--probably even harmful--why do educators call for even more of it? In all likelihood, punishment survives because of its symbolic significance, a sharp reminder that power to inflict discomfort is the right of the authoritarian teacher.

The Behavioral Psychology Approach

A second approach to school discipline is found in the principles of behavioral psychology. Although B. F. Skinner is generally credited with the seminal research in developing this theory of "operant conditioning," earlier thinkers, dating as far back as John Locke, have contributed to the principles embraced by this approach. According to Locke, and later to

Skinner and his followers, power resides not so much in authority figures as in the external environment in terms of the rewards that a person receives for certain behaviors.

In his well-known Walden Two, Skinner has his persona Frazier set forth the basic tenets of behaviorism:

> ...If it is in our power to create any of the situations which a person likes or to remove any situation he doesn't like, we can control his behavior. When he behaves as we want him to behave, we simply create a situation he likes or remove one he doesn't like. As a result, the probability that he will behave that way again goes up, which is what we want. Technically, it's called positive reinforcement. The old school made the amazing mistake of supposing the opposite was true, that by removing a situation a person likes or setting up one he doesn't like--in other words, by punishing him--it was possible to reduce the possibility that he would behave in a given way again. That simply doesn't hold....[11]

In his deterministic view of conditioned behavior, "the environment takes over the role function and role of autonomous man... [and] the fact remains that it is the environment which acts upon the perceiving person, not the perceiving person who acts upon the environment."[12]

The shared assumptions of behaviorists include these:

·Power resides in the contingencies and consequences of behavior. To control behavior a teacher needs to know what rewards (reinforces) a student's behavior so that the reward can be arranged as a consequence of the desired behavior. All behavior is learned.

·Positive reinforcement is the most powerful shaper of human behavior. Teachers who provide concrete rewards (e.g., food), activity rewards (e.g., running errands), and social rewards (e.g., field trips) as payoffs for specified behaviors (e.g., no chatter) can increase "desired" behavior.

•Directing their behavior toward reaching specific goals in small steps of accomplishment is the pivotal value for children to learn. Programmed learning operates on this principle.

•Punishment is of little educational worth, except to suppress behaviors that are clearly harmful to the student. Punishment may weaken an existing behavior but does not teach a substitute behavior.

•Because power is in the external environment, student misbehavior must be analyzed in terms of the rewards it brings the child. Scientific techniques of identifying and scheduling the rewards that modify behavior are under the control of the teacher-as-behavioral engineer.

•Students are always the end product of their conditioned responses and thus have no real freedom.

The teacher who adopts the behavioral approach frequently asks such questions as: "What will motivate this student? Am I using sufficient verbal and non-verbal praise and reinforcement? How am I unwittingly rewarding undesirable behavior?" Specific behavioral strategies include the following:

(1) Behaviors should be systematically analyzed and charted on "base lines." In many cases, students can be taught (and motivated by) the activity of charting their own behavior improvement.

(2) Rewards should be established in accordance with the needs and interests of the students whose behavior is being modified. (Actually all learning for a behaviorist is the modification of behavior.) Rewards should be paired with and immediately follow the target behavior to be strengthened (reinforced). As the behavior becomes more frequent over time, the rewards should be spaced at greater intervals on an intermittent schedule. Students can be taught to

83

associate secondary reinforcers (praise, for example) with primary reinforcers (food, for example), eventually substituting the secondary for the primary.

(3) As the behavioral engineer, the teacher must be ever alert to environmental contingencies that shape behavior. Arranging the environment so that it produces rewards for desired behavior will control discipline problems over time.

(4) A teacher's power flows from a knowledge of the techniques of behavior modification: positive reinforcement, negative reinforcement, token economies, principles of extinction and satiation, modeling desirable behavior, and teaching cues or "prompts," for example. Teachers who apply such principles work at "catching the child being good" before giving attention or praise (positive reinforcement). If a student is disruptive, he may be sent to a "time-out" area until he can decide to behave appropriately (negative reinforcement). If a teacher has a student who throws paper at the waste can, the student can be required to stay after school to throw a few hundred more (satiation). To keep a group quietly at work, the teacher may tiptoe around the room, whispering to individuals (modeling).

Behaviorists, then, see power as a force vested in the operant conditioning process, itself always operating in the shaping of human behavior. The teacher who knows what is rewarding to given students can use that knowledge as a force to change behavior. Rewards, however, have to be skillfully arranged to be powerful reinforcers. Knowing how to pair rewards with target behaviors and how to time these rewards is crucial in effective "behavior management." Power for the teacher, consequently, is a result of the systematic and scientific techniques of training as that procedure can be "applied" to students. Finally, power for the behaviorist derives from the manipulation of consequences (pleasant and unpleasant) in terms of primary needs (e.g., food) and secondary needs (e.g., approval) of students. Thus, power to effect orderly behavior requires the teacher to employ the knowledge and techniques of the experimental psychologist in the classroom.

The behaviorist offers some alternatives to the unproductive and harmful punishment practices of the authoritarian. Managing discipline becomes a clinical, scientific process when one locates power in the external environment, the contingencies of behavior. This systematic objectification of control--through the techniques of reinforcement theory--minimizes personal power struggles between student and teacher, since the teacher's concern is not so much one of commanding respect as it is determining what consequences can be arranged that will reinforce an individual student or an entire class. To control the environment is, indirectly, to control student behavior. The emphasis on rewards accentuates positive experiences for students, thus mitigating the negativism of punishment.

Still, there are serious social and ethical questions about behavior modification as a unilateral approach to school discipline. The Skinnerian vision of an engineered society which "shifts the determination of behavior from autonomous man to the environment"[13] suggests a totalitarian, psychologist-controlled social order potentially more authoritarian and manipulative than any police state. Abuses by teachers in the inhumane use of "aversives" (e.g., electric shocks) and "time-out" rooms (e.g., locked closets) raise doubts about educational practices growing out of behavior modification techniques. Even the reliance on extrinsic positive rewards such as candy and toys as a major control strategy is open to serious criticism. The line between rewards and bribery is not easy to establish.

Furthermore, the implications of a depersonalized, deterministic, and mechanistic educational process where children are "shaped" toward pre-established behavioral objectives may result in a limited concept of learning and discipline. Behaviorists tend to define away such aspects of humanity as creativity, intuition, insight, freedom, and valuing because these are internal subjective states that do not lend themselves easily to objectification and scientific control. When power to determine behavior exists in the external environment, the subjective and affective dimensions are relatively insignificant to a pedagogical theory.

The Human Relations Approach

A third approach to contemporary discipline

problems in schools is based on principles of humanistic education advocated by a variety of psychologists, philosophers, and educators. Many of these writers--such as Carl Rogers, Arthur Combs, William Glasser, and Thomas Gordon--are reacting against some of the values and strategies of behaviorism. This diverse group tends to see emerging school discipline problems as a consequence of poor classroom community and communication, weak self-concepts, and personal problems of students. Other shared assumptions include these:

- Power resides within individuals; therefore, the aim of education is to help each student develop personal powers and interpersonal skills to maximize human potential.

- Relationships should be personal and relatively egalitarian rather than official, hierarchical, and role-specific.

- Independence and self-worth are among the most important values that schools should develop in students.

- Punishment should be replaced by social contracts, logical consequences, conferences, and problem solving sessions.

- Because power resides in students, the teacher's role is to "facilitate" the growth and proper exercise of student power. Students are encouraged to be active participants in establishing classroom rules.

- Freedom, like power, resides in the student as a human right. The teacher attempts to help students use their freedom constructively in accordance with democratic principles.

The humanistic educator has great faith in students to solve their own discipline and learning difficulties. Carl Rogers characterizes this attitude when he says:

> Human beings have a natural potential for learning. They are curious about their world, they are eager to develop and learn, and have the capacity for

> making constructive discriminations
> between learning opportunities. This
> potentiality for learning, for dis-
> covery, can be released under suitable
> conditions....In short, the student's
> desire to learn can be trusted....Self-
> initiated learning, involving the whole
> person of the learner--feelings as well
> as intellect--is the most pervasive and
> lasting.[14]

The teacher who employs the human relations approach tends to ask such questions as: "What is
creating this problem for my students? How can I
understand the frustrations which intefere with their
healthy growth? Can the class as a whole cooperate
in the solution of our shared problems?

Specific techniques growing out of this general
approach to school discipline include these:

(1) Rules should be mutually arrived at as part
of the social contract of the democratic classroom.
Curwin and Mendler suggest the following procedure:

> We feel it is beneficial [for the
> teacher] to assume the role of a
> group member, while maintaining
> control to see that the decision-
> making process works effectively.
> However, you will ultimately have
> to live by the contract and be re-
> sponsible for its implementation....
> As a way of avoiding mistrust we en-
> courage you to go along with as many
> rules and consequences as possible
> which are agreed to by the class....
> attempt to reach unanimous consensus.[15]

Negotiated rules teach students how to share power in
the classroom.

(2) Logical consequences should replace punishments. Students can help determine these consequences
when engaged in rule-setting. As Dreikurs explains:
"There is a fine line of distinction between punishment and consequences. The child quickly recognizes
the difference. Natural consequences express a logical
and immediate result of the transgression, not imposed

on him by an authority, but by the situation itself, by
reality."[16] To send a child to the office for breaking
his desk is punishment; requiring him to come back after school to help repair the desk is a logical consequence.

(3) Communication techniques should be employed
to help students identify their problems and solve
them. Here teachers can use Rogerian counseling--de-
signed to reflect the feelings of students rather than
to judge them. Gordon advocates such "communication
facilitators" as passive listening, acknowledgement responses, door openers, and "active" listening.[17] The
teacher is free to express his or her own feelings
through "I messages," which do not attack or punish
students as the cause of the teacher's angry feelings.

(4) Affective approaches should be employed to
develop feelings, values, and morals. As Combs argues,
"Empathic teachers, honestly concerned with understanding how students think, feel, and perceive, are far
more likely than other teachers to be liked by their
students [and] have less problems with motivation and
discipline...."[18] Techniques such as values clarification, values analysis, and moral dilemmas can help
develop the valuing and decision making capabilities of
students.

Humanistic teachers, then, see power as potentiality, vested in humans who can develop in directions of
autonomy, freedom, and responsibility (both personal
and social). Teachers cannot use power in a coercive
or manipulative fashion and expect to promote growth;
they can, however, help students release (or realize)
their own powers of learning, growing, deciding.
Thomas Gordon describes this humanistic concept of
power:

> — Power never influences. Coercion by a
>   powerful teacher never educates or per-
>   suades a student. He simply chooses
>   whether to submit, fight, or withdraw
>   until the power pressure is off. So
>   teachers who use power actually lessen
>   Their influence as transmitters of
>   values...."[U]ncontrollable" students
>   don't need more or better external
>   controls. They need internal controls

88

and these come only from relationships in which their needs--as well
as those with whom they relate--are
respected.[19]

Thus, power for the humanistic educator is human potential itself, which should be nurtured in students by
giving them responsibility, support, and communication
skills to promote individual self-development and
human relations in the classroom community.

The human relations model offers some alternatives
to punishment not found in the repertoire of the authoritarian or the behaviorist. The more personal
approach to students has potential for building supportive, rather than subservient or clinical, relationships between students and between students and teacher. Concern for communication, feelings, and values
can mitigate antagonism and power struggles in the
classroom. Respecting and nurturing the independence
and active participation of students in the social
contract of the miniature community are educational
activities consistent with the democratic principles
of the larger society. Surely, helping students to
learn how to make decisions (and take responsibility
for the consequences) and how to evaluate the moral
implications of decisions and behaviors can shift responsibility for discipline to students themselves--as
maturing, responsible human beings.

On the other hand, there are many practical problems in this approach as it relates to school discipline. It takes teachers of unusual talent and personality to make the approach work. The bureaucratic,
factory-model school with large classes works against
the slow processes of personal rapport and community
solidarity. Pressures for academic/cognitive achieve-
ment--exacerbated by back-to-basics trends--de-
emphasize the affective aspects of humanistic education. The ephemeral and passe open education movement,
which espoused similar goals in the 1960s, hardly
augers renewed emphasis on values education in the
austere 1980s. Besides, humanistic education has
always been more appealing in theory than in practice.
Evidence, for example, that values clarification or
moral reasoning programs actually reduce school discipline problems is scant. The forces of contemporary
society do not point toward an imminent revolution to
sweep humanistic education into the public school

system.

Toward a Pedagogical Approach to Discipline

My analysis of three general approaches to problems of school discipline has been intended as an assessment of the strengths and weaknesses of these approaches, and I have tried to show some parallel relationships between educational assumptions of each approach and corresponding practices advocated by proponents. Matters of pedagogy and punishment relate to the locus of power in each general model of education examined: authoritarians locate power in hierarchical offices and roles; behaviorists, in the environment surrounding the "actor"; and humanistic educators, inside the individual and within his or her classroom community.

In large measure, one's approach to school discipline will be determined by where he or she thinks (or assumes) power over human behavior resides. While such a conclusion may clarify some of the school discipline debate, it falls short of a prescription for solutions to this major--and seemingly intractable--dilemma in contemporary education. Ultimately, educators and society itself, must create a coherent and (in my opinion) multi-faceted approach to school discipline that draws upon the best aspects of existing theory and practice.

The development of an integrated and eclectic pedagogical approach to school discipline requires educators to redefine basic assumptions about education and discipline, which might include the following new assumptions:

·Power resides in institutions and offices, in the external environment, and in individuals and communities. Teachers need to know where power over human action is in order to employ it for educational and social change.

·Educational relationships are based on roles, capacity to reinforce behavior, and personal interactions. Teachers need to understand the complex ways in which they relate to students as authority figures, managers of instruction and behavior, and human beings.

90

·Education is concerned with a wide variety of values, both traditional and emerging. Teachers need to know how to help students understand, evaluate, and act on personal and social values.

·Punishment has its proper uses in educational contexts but must be evaluated against such alternatives as positive reinforcement and social contracts. Teachers need to be able to employ disciplinary measures that are both theoretically and practically appropriate in given situations and that are consistent with a teacher's philosophy of education.

·Because power is distributed in several places (rather than focused in one), teachers need to be able to analyze the dynamics of power and its implications for instruction and discipline. Discipline is inextricably an aspect of instruction.

·Students in school have freedom as humans, but there are constraints on freedom that grow out of role relationships and environmental restrictions. Teachers need to know how to use instruction and the social milieu of the classroom to teach students responsible uses of freedom. Student rights are balanced by student responsibilities; individual freedoms cannot ignore social obligations.

The specific applications of a wide variety of discipline techniques may be found in every public school: rules, token economies, time-out rooms, social contracts, behavior clinics, and problem solving sessions, for example. Most teachers probably know what their orientations to discipline are--whether toward the authoritarian end of the power continuum or toward the humanistic side. This article has been designed, in part, to help teachers clarify and expand that knowledge. Indeed, fragmented and incoherent discipline practices--varying from teacher to teacher and school to school--and poorly developed philosophies of discipline can hardly be expected to result in effective school-wide policies and practices.

What is essential for effective practice in dealing with discipline is an integrated and fully developed philosophy of school discipline, one built on the kind of broad platform suggested here for the pedagogical model. Only when teachers and (even) total school faculties have evolved a mature and comprehensive approach--well grounded in research and theory--can we expect to see lasting solutions to the discipline problem in our public schools. Of course, we need to have room for diversity and flexibility of management techniques within schools; but hit-and-miss practices in handling discipline will not, in the final analysis, improve the teacher's lot. As John Dewey once noted, there is nothing so practical as a good theory. The most practical first step for teachers who want to improve school discipline is to develop a good theoretical knowledge of various approaches to this general problem. The concept of power is a useful one for developing such knowledge.

Education--both its ends and means--has always been characterized by diversity within a shifting, evolving, loosely-defined consensus of our society. The task before us in solving the school discipline problem is (1) to analyze the potential contributions to a workable consensus, (2) to develop a comprehensive model--what I have called "The Pedagogical Approach"--that is a workable synthesis of the more limited competing models now available,[20] and (3) to implement this comprehensive model wherever possible.

Although this present discussion has only dealt with the first task area of analysis, I am confident that we can complete the final two steps in the near future. That prospect is an exciting one indeed.

FOOTNOTES

1. In a Senate subcommittee report in 1975, Senator Birch Bayh said that violence and vandalism in the nation's schools yearly amounts to more than one-half billion dollars, 100 murders, 12,000 armed robberies, over 200,000 assaults on teachers and students, and more than 250,000 burglaries. See Our Nation's Schools--A Report Card (Washington, D.C.: U.S. Congress, Senate Committee on Judiciary, April 1975).

2. The Gallup Poll, as reported in the September 1979 *Phi Delta Kappan*, indicated that for the tenth time in the last eleven years school discipline is perceived by the public as education's most important problem.

3. See, for example, Rudolf Dreikurs et al., *Maintaining Sanity in the Classroom* (New York: Harper and Row, 1971); Charlotte Epstein, *Classroom Management and Teaching* (Reston, Va.: Reston Publishing Company, 1979); Eugene Howard, *School Discipline Desk Book* (West Nyack, N.Y.: Parker Publishing Company, 1979); Margaret Maggs, *The Classroom Survival Book: A Practical Manual for Teachers* (New York: New Viewpoints, 1980).

4. See, for example, S. Reed, "What You Can Do To Prevent Teacher Burnout," *The National Elementary Principal*, March 1979; Andrew DuBrin et al., "Teacher Burnout: How To Cope When Your World Goes Black," *Instructor*, January 1978; B. Hendrickson, "Teacher Burnout: How To Recognize It, What To Do About It," *Learning*, January 1979; C. Ronald Brown and Patrick Carlton, "How to Conquer Stress When You Can and Cope With It When You Can't," *The National Elementary Principal*, March 1980.

5. The following definition captures the essence of the concept: "Social power is (a) the potentiality (b) for inducing forces (c) in other persons (d) toward acting or changing in a given direction." Ronald Lippitt et al., "The Dynamics of Power," in *Group Dynamics: Research and Theory*, ed. Dorwin Cartwright and Alvin Zander (Evanston, IL.: Row & Peterson, 1960).

6. Richard Christie and Marie Jahoda, eds., *Studies in the Scope and Method of "The Authoritarian Personality"* (Glencoe, IL.: Free Press, 1954).

7. Mary Lynn Crow and Merle E. Bonney, "Recognizing the authoritarian Personality Syndrome in Educators," *Phi Delta Kappan*, September 1975, p. 42.

8. James Dobson, *Dare To Discipline* (Wheaton, IL.: Tyndale House, 1970), p. 27.

9. Frederick Jones, "The Eye Contact Method," *Instructor*, November 1978, p. 64.

10. As quoted by Robert J. Trotter in "This is Going To Hurt You More Than It Hurts Me," *Science News*, November 1972, p. 332. See also Roosevelt Ratliff, "Physical Punishment Must Be Abolished," *Educational Leadership*, March 1980, pp. 474-76.

11. B. F. Skinner, *Walden Two* (Toronto: The Macmillan

Company, 1948), pp. 259-60.

12. B. F. Skinner, <u>Beyond Freedom</u> and <u>Dignity</u> (New York: Alfred A. Knopf Inc., 1971), pp. 176, 178-79.

13. <u>Ibid</u>., p. 205.

14. Carl Rogers, "The Facilitation of Significant Learning," in <u>The Psychology of Open Teaching</u> and <u>Learning</u>, ed. Melvin Silberman et al. (Boston: Little, Brown and Company, 1972, pp. 278-79.

15. Richard Curwin and Allen Mendler, <u>The Discipline Book: A Complete Guide to School</u> and <u>Classroom Management</u> (Reston, Va.: Reston Publishing Company, 1980), pp. 132-33.

16. Rudolf Dreikurs, <u>Psychology in the Classroom</u> (New York: Harper and Row, 1968), p. 75.

17. Thomas Gordon, <u>TET: Teacher Effectiveness Training</u> (New York: Peter H. Wyden, 1974), pp. 61-64.

18. Arthur W. Combs, "Humanistic Goals of Education," in <u>Humanistic Education Sourcebook</u>, ed. Donald Read and Sidney Simon (Englewood Cliffs, N.J.: Prentice-Hall, 1975), p. 97.

19. Gordon, <u>TET</u>, p. 215.

20. For two new texts that attempt a synthesis see Curwin and Mendler, <u>The Discipline Book</u>, and Charles Wolfgang and Carl Glickman, <u>Solving Discipline Problems: Alternative Strategies for Classroom Teachers</u> (Boston: Allyn and Bacon, 1980). See also Thomas R. McDaniel "Exploring Alternatives to Punishment," <u>Phi Delta Kappan</u>, March 1980 and "Principles of Classroom Discipline: Toward a Pragmatic Synthesis," <u>The Clearing House</u>, December 1977.

EXPLORING ALTERNATIVES TO PUNISHMENT:

THE KEYS TO EFFECTIVE DISCIPLINE

The Problem

Beginning teachers, and experienced teachers too, are acutely aware of the importance--and the difficulty--of maintaining good classroom discipline. The public, by declaring school discipline as the number one problem in American education in every Gallup Poll in this decade, joins professional educators in the recognition of this major problem. Indeed, the most recent Gallup analysis (as reported in the September 1979 Phi Delta Kappan) points out that "one person in four names discipline as the most important problem" and that "either the public schools have found no way to deal effectively with this problem or the public is not yet aware of measures that are being tried." No wonder Dreikurs and Cassel contend, "Presently our school system is in a dilemma regarding discipline. The controversy over punishment can not be resolved unless we give teachers alternative effective techniques for dealing with children who misbehave and refuse to learn."[1]

While the Supreme Court recently refused to agree that corporal punishment was a violation of the Constitution's "cruel and unusual punishment" prohibition in the Eighth Amendment,[2] almost all of the research extant suggests that corporal punishment--indeed, any form of punishment--is unhelpful at best and at worst absolutely counterproductive to good discipline. A panel of the American Psychological Association in 1972 asserted that "physical violence imprinted at an early age and the modeling of violent behavior by punishing adults induces habitual violence in children."[3] As early as 1938 B. F. Skinner found in animal experiments that punishment (or aversive stimuli) does no more than to temporarily extinguish a response while creating fear and hostility in the process.

In spite of research, pronouncements by the APA and the ACLU, and heavy liability to teachers who harm students through corporal punishment,[4] punishment continues to be the staple of discipline procedures in all too many schools. Corporal punishment has been banned in Poland since 1783, in the Netherlands since

1850, in France since 1887, in Finland since 1890, and in Sweden since 1958. Most Communist countries, including the Soviet Union, do not allow corporal punishment in public schools.[5] And yet in the United States 40 states authorize corporal punishment in schools while only Massachusetts and New Jersey disallow the practice by state law. Why does punishment continue to be used daily in American public schools? Tradition, increased school crime and violence, and the failure of school systems and teacher education programs to promote effective alternatives are the probable reasons that ineffective punishment practices prevail; but there are alternatives.

Alternatives

Educational theory and research--drawing from various schools of thought, philosophies, and psychological perspectives--have provided teachers with a multitude of principles and practices that are superior to punishment in establishing good school and classroom discipline. These approaches require skill and perseverance but have the potential for creating positive relationships, cooperation, and self discipline in students. While no more than a brief description is possible here, teachers are encouraged to investigate these alternatives to punishment in further detail and to incorporate into their disciplinary practices those alternative approaches which are most compatible with their teaching styles and personal philosophies.

The Behavioral Model

The techniques of behavior modification have grown out of operant conditioning experiments by psychologists over the past few decades. The behavioral approach suggests that behaviors, whether in the cognitive area or in the discipline area, are shaped by principles of reinforcement. Both positive and negative reinforcement are more effective in developing "desirable" student behavior than is punishment. Specific application of this approach to discipline suggests that the teacher should:

1. Catch-the-child being good and reward him. Many behavior problems result from a child's need for attention and his realization that teachers generally ignore behaving students to give attention to troublemakers. The squeaky wheel gets the grease. Reversing

the process by ignoring minor misbehavior to focus attention on cooperative children is a lesson soon learned by a class. The hardest part of this technique for the teacher is to be consistent, systematic, and doggedly patient. Rewards should immediately follow the appropriate behavior to be reinforced.

2. Establish rewards that children will work for and connect these directly to "desirable" behavior. Teachers can use questionnaires, classroom discussions, and observation of what children do in their free time (a technique called "premacking") to find out what things and activities children find rewarding. These rewards may then be paired with target behavior to strengthen the motivation of students to behave appropriately. Food, toys, free time, trips, comic books, conversation breaks, special jobs, games--these are only a few of the reinforcers that an imaginative teacher can use as rewards.[6] For bigger rewards use chips or markers as tokens which can, after accumulation to a specified number, be redeemed. (This is how grocery stores use green stamps to strengthen our tendency to shop at their places of business.)

3. Praise desirable behavior in the classroom by positive verbal and non-verbal responses. Research tells us that teachers do not use praise effectively and, in fact, use it far less than they _think_ they do. One large survey in a public school system in Florida, for example, found that 77 percent of the teachers' interactions with children were negative in tone.[7] Teachers need to expand their verbal praise list beyond the conventional "good," "yes," "right," and "OK" responses and to work at such non-verbal reinforcers as smiles, nods, touch, attention, closeness, gestures, and eye contact. Instead of writing names on the board of misbehaving students who are to "stay in" at recess or for detention hall, write up names of the _best_ behaved students. With a noisy class, put a check mark in a column on the board after every five minutes of quiet and give the whole class five minutes of free time if they earn, say, five checks during the period.

4. Use "modeling" to teach appropriate behavior. Since children imitate behavior, particularly that of significant others such as peer leaders and teachers, teachers can exemplify the behavior they expect from students. When teachers try to talk over an under-

current of classroom chatter, noisily walk around the room during a quiet-time seat work assignment, come to class late and unorganized, respond to "called-out" questions and comments, they are modeling the very behavior they most despair about in students. Teachers should not only model the kind of behavior they expect from students but should use well-behaved prestigious peers as group leaders, or in paired seating arrangements, to enhance their modeling value in the classroom.

5. Teach the cues that signal the approach of an expected behavior. Cueing can be one of the most effective techniques for eliminating situations that frequently result in punishment for children. While many teachers have developed--probably intuitively--a repertoire of cues, most teachers could benefit from a conscious, systematic, overt recognition that cues can be employed to create good behavior. A teacher may ring a small bell when it is time to change centers, turn the light switch on and off when it is time to put laboratory equipment away, stand before the class with a raised hand when attention is required, point to the lunch monitor when it is time to exit for lunch. But a creative teacher can go far beyond these obvious examples. In a restless and talkative class the students can be taught to cue the teacher that they know an answer by resting their heads on the desk. The teacher, of course, must then reinforce this behavior by recognizing such a student for the answer. Cues should be explained to students and consistently followed in the classroom.

6. Use negative reinforcement when a child's behavior is unacceptable. Unlike punishment, negative reinforcement allows the child to terminate an aversive situation when he is ready to behave. The distinction may be slight but it is important. Sending a misbehaving child to stand in the corner for "the rest of the period" is punishment; removing him from the group to a "time out" area "until he is ready to play by the rules" is negative reinforcement. In the first case a child can only reflect upon his sins while in the latter he can decide to change his behavior and in so doing remove the mildly aversive condition of solitary confinement. He is more likely in this negative reinforcement situation to develop positive behaviors whereas punishment usually generates resentment and revenge.

Because behavior modification techniques can be powerful, teachers must be sensitive to the ethical implications[8] and the practical consequences[9] of this approach.

The Human Relations Model

The human relations approach to school discipline rests on a number of psychological theories, such as those developed by Carl Rogers, Haim Ginott, Thomas Gordon, and William Purkey. Those who look at discipline from a human relations perspective propose a number of strategies that supercede the application of punitive measures. Emphasis is generally placed on communication, democratic processes, and personal interaction in the classroom. Practical application of theory suggests that the teacher should:

1. Treat students with respect and politeness. Ginott says, "A wise teacher talks to children the way he does to visitors at his home."[10] In what he calls "invitational teaching," William Purkey says the focus is "on the teacher's belief system--that students are valuable, can learn, and are responsible for their conduct. The teacher communicates these beliefs within a framework of gentle but firm expectations for each student."[11]

2. Communicate effectively by describing rather than evaluating. Ginott says, "sarcasm is not good for children. It destroys their self-confidence and self-esteem. . . . Verbal spankings do not improve performance or personality. . . . When a child feels aggrieved, it is best to acknowledge his complaint and voice his wish. . . . 'Talk to the situation, not to the personality and character' is the cardinal principle of communication."[12] Instead of verbal punishment--what Ginott calls naming, blaming, and shaming--teachers should develop the language of acceptance, "congruent communication," and brevity of speech.

3. Communicate effectively by reflecting feelings, a counseling technique developed by Rogers. Gordon outlines a hierarchy of "communication facilitators"--passive listening, acknowledgement responses, door openers, and active listening[13]--that enhances this communication skill. The essential task for the teacher-as-listener is to clarify and restate what his students are saying, giving expression to underlying

feelings that seem to be causing a student's anger, fear, or frustration. When a student challenges a teacher by saying, "I'm not going to take that stupid test now," a teacher using active listening would not respond by ordering, threatening, moralizing, or punishing; instead he would reflect what he thinks is the student's underlying feeling: "You are afraid you are not going to do well." Such a response keeps communication open, avoids "put down" messages, and avoids the usual power struggle in confrontations.

4. Communicate effectively by using "I-messages," a technique advocated by both Ginott and Gordon. The "I-message" allows a teacher to describe his own feelings--disappointment, fear, frustration--in such a way that students are not personally attacked or punished. It "avoids the negative impact that accompanies you-messages, freeing the student to be considerate and helpful, not resentful, angry, and devious."[14] These messages have minimal negative evaluation of students and do not injure personal relationships. According to Gordon, the "I-message" has three components: a description of the behavior that bothers the teacher, a statement of the tangible effects of that behavior, and the feeling that the teacher consequently has. For example: "When you have your feet in the isle [description of behavior], I am apt to trip over them [tangible effect], and I am afraid I will fall and get hurt [feeling]."[15] This kind of communication tends to strengthen human relations and reduces the conflicts and the roadblocks to communication that so frequently end in verbal or physical punishment for students.

5. Negotiate with students to establish rules of behavior and to find solutions to problems. William Glasser advocates the use of the classroom meeting to discuss and resolve community problems, and the "Glasser circle" is now used in many schools by teachers who are trying to involve students more responsibly in decision-making. As Dennis Van Avery argues, "the process of learning responsibility can best take place between people who can readily get to know each other. We need continually to be concerned about allowing small groups of young people to interact with responsible adults."[16] Gordon proposes a formal problem-solving process to deal with discipline and other shared problems in the classroom, a process that involves students in a democratic and creative way. The teacher

defines the problem and facilitates a brainstorming of possible solutions (all are listed on the board), which are then evaluated. The class then moves toward a consensus on the one solution that everyone, and that includes the teacher, is willing to try for a specified period of time.

Because the human relations approach requires an unusual range of skills and attitudes on the part of the teacher, a teacher's application of the techniques above should be developed carefully and patiently.

The Pedagogical Model

The pedagogical approach to discipline has grown out of the research of educators and the practice of teachers. Obviously, this approach has been influenced by both behavioral research and humanistic theory-- but the emphasis in the pedagogical model is on instructional practices and on specific interaction patterns between students and teachers. There has been no shortage of advice to teachers about how to discipline; however, the focus here is on how to discipline without punishing. Among the selected principles to consider are those that argue that the teacher should:

1. Keep discipline problems from occurring by providing structured but varied lessons. When lessons are student-centered, provide for active learning, and promote student-teacher shared planning, a good bit of the boredom and frustration that create discipline problems can be eliminated. Teachers who design purposeful, multi-activity plans and do so by incorporating high-interest materials are applying preventive discipline.[17]

2. Develop a repertoire of motivation techniques. Assigning projects to coincide with student interests, using "hands-on" learning experiences, making motivational statements, establishing rewards and prizes, providing for student choice wherever possible, employing instructional games, and showing personal interest in students and their educational accomplishments--all of these practices enhance student motivation. Of course, it is also important for the teacher himself to show involvement and enjoyment in the class activities to motivate by example.

3. Use voice control and distance management to

keep the tone and pace of a class on target. In this respect, a teacher should use the "soft reprimand" (rather than giving public attention to misbehaving students by using a loud reprimand), lower the voice and/or stop talking if an undercurrent of chatter develops (rather than trying to talk above the noise), employ pauses and voice inflection to assure voice variety. Further, the teacher should move <u>toward</u> individuals or small groups that are inattentive while moving <u>away</u> from students who are responding to a teacher's question. The teacher's proximity will tend to curtail inattention while moving away from the responder will encourage him to speak louder and across a larger number of students included in the increased "stage distance."

4. Find natural or logical consequences for student misbehavior. Rudolf Dreikurs, who argues for this approach to discipline in several of his texts, defines "natural consequences" as the "natural flow of events without interference of the teacher or parent. The child who refuses to eat will go hungry. The natural consequence of not eating is hunger." He defines "logical consequences" as "arranged or applied. If the child spills his milk, he must clean it up. In this situation the consequence is tied to the act."[18] If a child is late for class, asking him to make up the time at the end of the day is a logical consequence; having him copy pages from a dictionary is mere punishment. Because a child does not associate punishment with his action, but with the punisher, he does not change his behavior or attitude. A natural or logical consequence, however, teaches students the rational reality of misbehavior. When a child is inattentive as an assignment is given, do not repeat it; when a student writes on his desk, require him to scrub the desk clean; when an instructional game gets out of hand, call it off and return to less enjoyable routine work. But in each case be sure to stress the <u>connection</u> between the behavior and the consequence.[19] Natural and logical consequences make sense to the student and help him to learn from his mistakes.

5. Employ assertiveness training techniques when student compliance with requests is important. A teacher may occasionally need to be unusually clear and firm about a request to a misbehaving student, particularly when students are testing the limits of authority or are not convinced that a teacher means what he

says. Frederick Jones describes this approach:

> Being assertive is the key. Asser-
> tiveness is 95 percent body
> language. . . . First turn and face
> the child. If you're not willing to
> commit your body in that direction
> don't expect the child to respond. . . .
> [P]ut an edge on your voice and say
> the student's name in a straight,
> flat tone. Next, make eye contact. . . .
> Lean toward him. . . . Very slowly walk
> right up to his desk so your leg is
> touching it, stand and look at the
> child. Don't say anything, don't
> hurry. By that time most kids will
> fold.[20]

In "assertive teaching" it is particularly important to
stay with your request until you know you have made
your point, repeating your position or request and refusing to be diverted or ignored. This is what is
known as "the broken record" technique. William
Glasser's well-known theory of "Reality Therapy"
incorporates many assertive principles, such as "be
committed. Build in a way to check back. . . . Don't
accept excuses. . . . Never give up."[21]

There are, of course, countless other pedagogical
principles that can help the effective teacher avoid
confrontations and conflicts that may result in punishment and to find ways to deal with students in non-
punitive interactions.[22]

Conclusion

Because school discipline is a critical issue in
education and society today, effective ways of creating
healthy and happy classrooms must be an important concern of educators everywhere. It is unlikely that much
constructive learning and teaching can be found where
there is violence, disruption, apathy, and conflict
between students and teachers. But it is also unlikely
that we can expect administrative crackdowns on misbehavior, "get-tough" attitudes by school boards, or
harsh punishment by teachers to create positive learning
environments within school systems. The long-term
solution to the school discipline crises is a professional staff of educators--principals, counselors, and

teachers--who can work competently and humanely with students and with instruction to find alternatives to punishment.

To accomplish these ends a concentrated cooperative effort is essential. A few specific steps could move education into an action orientation to develop and disseminate effective discipline practices:

·Recommendation 1 - Educational researchers should move with alacrity to design and evaluate models of classroom management that integrate the most attractive aspects of existing models (such as the three described in this article). These should be metatheoretical models that draw from theory but point toward practice.

·Recommendation 2 - Teacher education institutions should develop courses in classroom management for pre-service teachers and inservice teachers. These should include as much observation, micro-teaching, and simulation as possible. Emphasis should be placed on practical strategies in the classroom.

·Recommendation 3 - School district personnel should create projects, perhaps in conjunction with universities, that are designed to involve teachers, principals, and supervisors in ongoing classroom and school-wide experimentation with innovative methods and techniques of management and instruction.

·Recommendation 4 - Professional organizations should emphasize classroom management by means of conferences and publications. Preventive discipline, home-school relations, motivation through subject matter, values education and the disruptive child, educational effects of punishment, causes of school violence--all of these need even more attention than they have so far received from the various associations of educators.

·Recommendation 5 - Local, state, and Federal levels of government should support efforts to get at the root of the discipline problem and to develop alternatives to punishment by providing funds for pilot projects and research at the various levels. Other forms of legislation and board action--e.g., to develop comprehensive discipline codes and policies, to create support services, and to establish consultant assistance to teachers and counselors--should be explored as well.

Clearly, these are inter-related enterprises and should be coordinated for maximum benefit. Sporadic efforts in all five areas can easily be found, but the imperative now is for increased cooperative effort. The problems of school discipline can not be quickly solved with band-aid techniques and superficial hit-and-miss methods. Because the underlying causes of our more serious discipline dilemmas, particularly in the inner cities, cut deeply into the social fabric of contemporary life, solutions depend ultimately on our ability to mend that fabric. Such a task belongs to the whole society, not to teachers alone. But teachers have a central role in this process. When teachers become skilled in the humane application of alternatives to punishment, those described here and others yet to be developed,[23] they can help schools become the kinds of places where students live and learn in well-regulated liberty.

FOOTNOTES

1. Rudolf Dreikurs and Pearl Cassel, Discipline Without Tears, 2nd ed., (New York: Hawthorn Books, 1972), p. 11.
2. The case, Ingraham v. Wright (1977) was decided on a close 5-4 split vote.
3. As quoted by Robert J. Trotter in "This is Going to Hurt You More Than it Hurts Me," Science News, November 18, 1972, p. 332.
4. For some of these liabilities see my "The Teacher's Ten Commandments: School Law in the Classroom," Phi Delta Kappan, June, 1979, pp. 703-708.
5. Tobyann Boonin, "The Benighted Status of U.S. School Corporal Punishment Practice," Phi Delta Kappan, January, 1979, p. 395.
6. Many recent texts in this area contain long lists of reinforcers along with explicit directions for scheduling rewards effectively. See, for example, J. Mark Ackerman, Operant Conditioning Techniques for the Classroom Teacher (Glenview, Illinois: Scott, Foresman and Co., 1972); John and Helen Krumboltz, Changing Children's Behavior (Englewood Cliffs, N.J.: Prentice-Hall, 1972); Charles and Clifford Madsen, Teaching Discipline: Behavioral Principles Toward a Positive Approach (Boston: Allyn and Bacon, 1970); James Walker and Thomas Shea, Behavior Modification: A Practical Approach for Educators (Saint Louis: The C. V. Mosby Co.,

1976); Charlotte Epstein, Classroom Management and
Teaching (Reston, Virginia: Reston Publishing
Company, 1979).

7. Bertram S. Brown, "Behavior Modification: What It
Is--and Isn't," Today's Education, January-February,
1976, pp. 67-68.

8. See, for example, Patricia Keir's "The Teacher as
Behavior Engineer," Educational Forum, November,
1977, pp. 111-117; and James D. Long and Virginia
H. Frye, Making It 'til Friday (Princeton:
Princeton Book Company, 1977, Chapter 8).

9. See, for example, David L. Gast and C. Michael
Nelson's "Time Out in the Classroom: Implications
for Special Education," Exceptional Children, April,
1977, pp. 461-464.

10. Haim Ginott, Teacher and Child (New York: The
Macmillan Company, 1972), p. 101.

11. William W. Purkey, Inviting School Success: A Self-
Concept Approach to Teaching and Learning (Belmont,
California: Wadsworth Publishing Company, 1978),
p. 57.

12. Ginott, pp. 66-84.

13. Thomas Gordon, TET: Teacher Effectiveness Training
(New York: Peter H. Wyden Publisher, 1974), pp. 61-
64.

14. Ibid., p. 139.

15. Ibid., p. 144.

16. Dennis Van Avery, "Contrasting Solutions for School
Violence," Phi Delta Kappan, November, 1975, pp.
177-178.

17. For other suggestions in this area see my "A Stitch
in Time: Principles of Preventive Discipline,"
American Secondary Education, June, 1979, pp. 52-57.
Also see Stanley A. Fagan and Nicholas J. Long,
"Before It Happens: Prevent Discipline Problems by
Teaching Self-Control," Instructor, January, 1976,
pp. 44-47.

18. Rudolf Dreikurs, et al., Maintaining Sanity in the
Classroom (New York: Harper and Row, Publishers,
1971), p. 80. See also his Logical Consequences:
A New Approach to Discipline (New York: Hawthorn
Press, 1968) and Discipline Without Tears (New York:
Hawthorn Press, 1972).

19. Don Dinkmeyer and Don Dinkmeyer, Jr., "Logical Consequences: A Key to the Reduction of Disciplinary
Problems," Phi Delta Kappan, June, 1976, pp. 665-
666.

20. Frederick Jones in "Instructor's Guide to Sanity-
Saving Discipline," Instructor, November, 1978,

p. 64. See also in the same article the contribution by Lee Canter, "Be an Assertive Teacher," p. 60.
21. William Glasser, "Ten Steps to Good Discipline," Today's Education, November-December, 1977, p. 61.
22. For some good practical suggestions see Dudley Shearburn's "What To Do When You See Red!" Teacher, September, 1977, pp. 90-91; Majorie L. Hipple, "Classroom Discipline Problems? Fifteen Humane Solutions," Childhood Education, February, 1978, pp. 183-187; Dorothy Rathbun, "How to Cope in the Middle School Jungle," Learning, November, 1977, pp. 40 ff; Leonard Burger, "Do You Referee When You Really Want to Teach?" Instructor, February, 1977, pp. 55-58.
23. One new approach that has promise is transactional analysis. See Ken Earnst, Games Students Play (Millbrae, California: Celestial Arts Publishing, 1972); Konstantinos and Constance Kravas, "Transactional Analysis for Classroom Management," Phi Delta Kappan, November, 1974, pp. 194-197; and Joseph D. Purdy, "How to Win at Uproar," Instructor, August-September, 1975, pp. 64-66.

IDENTIFYING DISCIPLINE PROBLEMS:

A SELF-EVALUATION EXERCISE

When it comes to classroom management in the elementary school, teachers often face a variety of problems with student behavior "types." Indeed, one of the reasons principles of school discipline seem to work so sporadically and unevenly is that the problems teachers face are as variable as the students they teach; yet there are certain typical behavior problems that bedevil every teacher. Below are described ten stereotypes of problem students that almost every teacher has encountered at some time in the classroom. Which characters do you think present the most severe discipline problems? Which the least? Before reading on, put each child on what you consider to be the appropriate step of the forced-choice discipline ladder:

Ten Problem Children

1) Clarence thinks he is the next Woody Allen. He seems to spend every working moment cracking jokes, guffawing loudly, and show-boating in class. If he can get a laugh at anyone's expense--including himself and the teacher--he will do so without hesitation. He's a regular clown.

2) Billy thinks he is the Godfather. His primary purpose in life is to demonstrate how tough he is. He has learned all sorts of tough cliches, postures, and rituals. He doesn't think too much about school or the teacher--certainly not in comparison with his macho image. Billy has been known to fight at the drop of a hat and has a particular fondness for terrorizing younger children. He is a first-class bully.

3) Sally must be working the third shift because she spends most of her school day sleeping. She doesn't bother the other kids; in fact, she is a loner. She is not only quiet and shy, she is listless and very rarely shows any interest in even your most enjoyable activities. Her quality of work is generally poor and she rarely does homework. Sally is your sleeper.

4) Brenda is always alert and cooperative. The problem is she is not very trustworthy and has a particular talent for apple-polishing. Whether or not

she is genuinely interested in your lesson, she will
tell you what an exciting lesson it was. She compli-
ments your appearance at least twice a day. Always,
she seems intent on manipulating you to her own
advantage and to getting special favors, permissions,
rewards, and attention. Brenda is a classic brown-
noser.

5) Bradley is immature. He sucks his thumb,
cries easily and often, whines and beggars like a two-
year old. You have the feeling he will have his thumb
in his mouth at age 20. He tends to hang around your
desk and needs an incredible amount of assistance doing
everything. He never remembers instructions. You know
he is insecure, and the other kids hold him in low regard in their social order. Frequently, he grabs on
to you and hovers in your footsteps. His nose is
always running; Bradley is a baby.

6) Sarah seems to have some latent hostility
toward adults. You have the feeling she is insulting
you in low whispers to her classmates while overtly
smiling at you. Several times you have suspected her
of devious and mischievous acts but you can never
prove it because she is wiley. Whatever she can get
away with--by fair means or foul--she will try. Sarah
is a sneak.

7) Sam is infuriating. A bright boy with a quick
wit, he is unbearably sassy. He thinks he is in a
personal duel with you but has judged himself the better
fighter. He has no respect for authority and his come-
back remarks are cutting and impertinent. You'd really
like to give him the back of your hand and wonder what
his parents do with his arrogant behavior. Sam is your
A-1 Smart Alec.

8) Chad seems totally without scruples. He seems
rather average on the surface but you have found that
you have to watch him carefully. Once he took everyone's best crayons leaving his dull, short, and broken
ones in return. He copies work from other kids whenever possible but always protests his innocence loudly
and profusely, even in the face of overwhelming
evidence. You wonder where he got his values and
whether or not he will stay out of jail in later life.
Chad is a cheat.

9) Blaze is old beyond her years. She had her

110

first real boy friend in kindergarten and she has been in the social whirl ever since. You are sure that she will be a social success in later life, but her total disregard of educational matters, her nonchalance about assignments and study, and haughty maturity--so young to be so jaded--are driving you bananas. You just don't seem to be able to communicate with her--maybe because she is just so blamed <u>blase</u>.

10) Harry is perpetual motion. He is always tapping on the desk with his fingers or pencil; he slides down in his chair, twists around, swings his arms like a helicopter, and frequently falls on the floor. He is always dropping things (usually at the worst time, making the most noise) and then making a big production about getting up and picking things up. His concentration span is very short and he can often be found wandering around the room. He creates a disturbance-- maybe because he is so <u>hyperactive</u>.

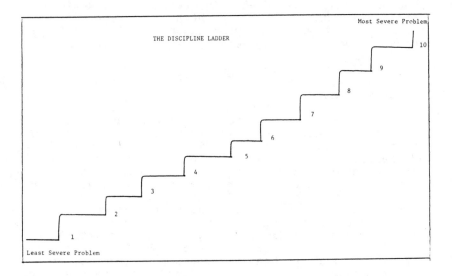

If you are like most teachers, you probably had Harry, Sam, Clarence, and Billy near the top of your ladder. These characters (frequently, but not always, boys) tend to be the most disruptive and threatening to the teacher's sense of control and order in the classroom. Dealing with these kinds of problems usually requires a teacher to have an unflappable sense of personal security, a well-structured classroom, and a persistent approach of personal contact. A sense of humor is also helpful here. Each of these characters seeks attention and recognition and any boring or slow-paced lesson will provoke their aggressive, high-energy behavior. The teacher who finds positive and constructive ways to meet these attention needs within the legitimate goals of the instructional program will tend to be successful with the hyperactive child, smart-alec, clown, and bully.

On the other hand, if you had students like Sarah, Bradley, and Chad at the top of your ladder, you probably have a low tolerance for dependent-passive students. Children with these kinds of behaviors (sneak, baby, cheat) usually have poor self-concepts and feelings of inferiority. Teachers may find success with these kids by providing personalized teacher encouragement, low-threat/high-success instructional strategies, and pairing with high ego strength students for activities. Praising only their acceptable behavior will also be useful in many cases.

If you had Sally, Brenda, and Blaze at the top of your ladder, you are in a minority of teachers. These three students (frequently, but not always, girls) are least disruptive in the classroom but are, nonetheless, discipline problems. Students who manifest these kinds of behaviors have found ways to cope with their inabilities and/or lack of interest in the classroom in "acceptable" ways. But it is probably better to think of students' discipline problems in terms of the effect of their behavior on their learning and social growth rather than on your teaching and peace of mind. A wise teacher will be as concerned about the sleeper and brown-noser as the bully, for each is failing to reach maximum potential in learning. Each, in short, lacks discipline. These students need to be instructionally challenged and personally counseled in order to change their motivations and behavioral styles. Helping such students to understand the various causes for their behavior is particularly important.

And what if your rankings violate all of the above grouping patterns? Then you are probably acutely aware that students in actuality come in an infinite variety of types and each poses a special problem for the

teacher. (Some extreme cases, of course, may require
help from counselors, psychologists, and other
personnel.) In the final analysis, each student has
to be taken on his own terms, encouraged, nurtured,
counseled, directed, socialized, individualized if he
is to develop a mature, self-discipline and a healthy
self-concept. Dealing with discipline is part and
parcel of the art of teaching: it comes with the
territory.

SO YOU WANT GOOD CLASSROOM BEHAVIOR?

DON'T PREACH IT--TEACH IT!

When I was in the third grade our teacher told us,
"I only have one rule in this classroom: Be Good."
Now, that sounded reasonable to most of us, I am sure,
but no one really had the vaguest idea what the rule
meant. It wasn't long, however, before little Grady
Fox (he is about six feet four now) pushed Bobby Rust
away from the gerbil cage and our teacher exclaimed,
"Grady, you know the rule and that isn't being good!"
Soon after that a group of girls were chattering while
our teacher was trying to explain something and again
she cautioned: "Girls, remember the rule." And so it
went.

By Christmas we had learned what "Be Good" meant
and, in fact, had discovered that our teacher had not
one rule but about twenty, such as:

Do not push other children away from the gerbil
cage;

Do not talk to your classmates while the teacher
is talking;

Do not come in from recess late;

Do not copy from your neighbor;

Do not break into the lunch line out of turn.

Somehow or other we eventually learned what our teacher
expected in the way of behavior. We also learned that
if we could not "be good" we were in for a lecture on
proper behavior and possibly some punishment when we
did not predict her hidden rules very successfully.

Now, my third grade teacher was really quite good
as a teacher, but I am convinced that she created
trouble for herself that could have been prevented. In
the first place, she could have made her hidden rules
clear, explicit, and specific at the outset. Since we
never knew specific prohibitions in advance, our class
had to go through a rather painful and inefficient
trial-and-error learning experience. Our teacher spent
a lot of time putting out fires and defining her

115

standards ex post facto. This probably led us (and her) to some resentment and frustration and may have led us to question the fairness of retributive justice. In the second place, our attempts (mostly subconscious, I am sure) to get clarification and definition of behavioral standards no doubt encouraged us to send up trial balloons--how were we to know what we could get away with if we didn't give it a try? In the third place, our teacher was always in a position of punishing and preaching which put her into a negative and often adversary relationship with her students. Teachers today need to be able to employ positive approaches to classroom discipline, to teach rather than preach the acceptable behavior that is desired, and to begin this process with youngsters as soon as they begin their schooling.

My thesis is that discipline is not something we can simply assume or demand, it is not automatic, but it can and should be taught in the kindergarten and elementary school. There is no point in lamenting the failure of all too many parents to instill "good" behavior and high standards of conduct in their off-spring, nor is it useful to complain that "I was hired to teach, not be a policeman." The kids are there in your classroom and the better able you are to teach kids the skills of deportment the happier you all will be.

Of course, if you have well-planned, well-motivated, multi-activity lessons; if you have suffi-cient structure, variety, and pacing; if you establish cordial and positive personal relationships with students within an efficient and business-like frame-work; if you use verbal and non-verbal reinforcement and a variety of rewards; and if you work hard to improve your classroom climate and control--you will have the elements of an effective discipline system. But in addition to these general principles of disci-pline teachers need to teach the skills of behavior in much the same way that other skills are taught to children. Below is a series of steps to take in teaching a given behavior.

First, determine the specific behaviors that you plan to teach. Be specific and descriptive rather than general and moralistic. Do not choose "be good" or even "don't cheat" since both are very broad and open to many definitions. Think, rather, in such terms as "test-taking behavior." Write down the behavior for yourself and (in most cases) for the benefit of your students. This step will provide specificity and descriptive clarity to ensure good communication among all members of the class and the teacher.

Second, discuss the behavior with your class in an objective and instructional format. There should be no attempt to be judgmental, authoritarian, or threatening: Not "if you don't, I'll . . ." but "we need to learn how to take a test."

Third, model the behavior you expect. Children can be taught much more effectively by example than by abstract verbal generalizations. If you will show them, even in a simulated example, the behavior they are to learn, your chances for success will improve. Here you can sit down, put all books away, pick up the test, and quietly begin your study of the questions. Model the kind of posture, concentration, and demeanor that you want the children to emulate.

Fourth, put the students through a practice session, a mock test in this case. This role playing is important in helping students internalize certain values and develop certain habits. At this stage you would separate chairs and provide other logistical arrangements that promote concentration and minimize cheating.

Fifth, teach the students the cues you will use to prompt or remind them of the behavior that is required. For example teach the class that if anyone forgets to concentrate on his own work, you will call his name quietly, and point alternately to your eye and hand as a reminder to keep his eyes on his own handiwork. Teaching cues is a crucial element in teaching behavior.

Sixth, apply the learnings above systematically at the earliest opportunity to enhance the transfer of learning to the real life situation in the classroom. Remember that young children have difficulty distinguishing between "cooperating" and "cheating" and that your purpose is to teach them the difference. After the real test show your appreciation for--that is, reinforce--the good test-taking behavior the class (or particular children) exhibited.

I have made the steps above seem time-consuming and overly elaborate when in fact they are neither. They do require some practice and patience but eventually will become second nature to both teacher and student. The important factors are the attitude of the teacher and the clarity of the specific behaviors being taught. Although I have used test-taking behavior as my example, such behaviors as coming into the classroom, working in groups, putting materials and equipment away, and exiting from the classroom can be taught in the same manner.

When teachers approach classroom behavior as an instructional challenge--and work to identify, model, practice, execute, and reinforce these behavioral skills--they will be teaching students important lessons of conduct for the classroom and society.

HOW TO BE AN EFFECTIVE AUTHORITARIAN:

A BACK-TO-BASIC APPROACH TO CLASSROOM DISCIPLINE

There has been, in recent years, a plethora of models, theories, and approaches to school discipline and classroom management.[1] Teachers are urged to be humanistic or behavioristic, to use logical consequences or classroom circle discussions, to reflect feelings, use "I-messages," or negotiate behavior contracts. Furthermore, philosophers and psychologists in education keep pointing out the limitations of a negative approach to classroom conflict and the legal/educational pitfalls in corporal punishment.[2] Although all this contemporary interest in and contribution to the discipline issue in public schools is desirable--and certainly useful--the basic problem of the teacher's orientation and experience in an authoritarian system has been grossly underestimated and misunderstood by those who would ameliorate classroom conflict.

Whether one can successfully implement various approaches to classroom management of behavior depends primarily on: a) the personal philosophy, values, experience of the teacher and b) the educational philosophy and role expectations held by the school. It is true that both a) and b) are subject (one would hope) to change and improvement, but at any point each is a given in the dynamics of discipline. I believe that most schools and most teachers are authoritarian-- by nature, necessity, tradition, and definition. If this assessment is valid, then it may follow that the best way to deal immediately and successfully with discipline problems is to help teachers become effective authoritarians, carrying out their assigned responsibilities for maintaining order and peace in the classroom. Perhaps at this point a definition and defense of authoritarian education is in order.

Authoritarians, unfortunately, have been too often stereotyped negatively. The very term now connotes severe, unfeeling, scowling oppression. Crow and Bonney draw this unflattering characature of such a teacher:

> . . . The authoritarian often views
> the classroom and his position in it
> as a source of almost unlimited power.

119

> He may view students as objects to
> be manipulated, used, or bullied. . . .
> He probably has little patience with
> the concept of allowing students to
> voice an opinion different from his
> own. . . . He places an inordinately
> high value on order, routine, and
> discipline.[3]

But such characterizations are no more fair to
authoritarians than are the extreme characterizations of
open education teachers as permissive and weak. For
example, an authoritarian can be firm with students
without being a "bully" or can value order without
placing an "inordinately high value" on this condition.

Indeed, the authoritarian teacher is merely one who
accepts the traditional role of the authority in the
classroom. He knows that society expects teachers to
be mature and responsible leaders, to pass on the
cultural heritage, to develop values of respect and
discipline in the young. The authoritarian teacher
understands that there are standards of behavior and
performance which need to be enforced if students are
to benefit from instruction. Even more surely, he
knows that an orderly society is dependent upon students who have learned the rule of law, one of the major
values of a democratic society.

It can be argued that the authoritarian teacher is
particularly sensitive to the built-in hierarchical
power structures of modern schools and contemporary
society. Indeed, research suggests that authoritarian
personalities naturally gravitate toward those social
institutions--the military, government, the ministry,
and education--where superior-inferior role relationships are most evident. Public schools are structured
so that power resides in well-defined offices. Students
are responsible to teachers who are responsible to
principals who are responsible to superintendents who
are responsible to boards of education. That is the
nature of a school, and teachers by definition must
exercise the authority of their office. This is their
major responsibility as an employee of the school
system.

In fact, the public school is (to use John Dewey's
oft quoted analogy) an "embryonic community," reflecting

many of the values of the larger society. Although the American society has sometimes been concerned with the process of democratization--Dewey's era might be one example, the chaotic 1960's another--it is clear that the Reagan era is returning us to those traditional values of stability, order, respect for authority that have always undergirded the conservative nature of our institutions, particularly schools. As Jenny Gray reminds us:

> . . . From the moment he signs a con-
> tract the teacher shares with the
> public school a tacit obligation to
> society. In the main we allow our-
> selves to be governed by duly elected
> persons and their representatives.
> This is the only way our society can
> function in an orderly way. It is
> not good, therefore, that our young
> people become adept at the fine art
> of insurrection. The teacher who
> allows students to victimize him in
> his classroom indirectly encourages
> them to victimize the man at the
> newstand, the stranger in the park,
> and the cop on his beat.[4]

The school is indeed a microcosm of the world outside.

Now, if in fact most schools and most teachers are authoritarian, what sorts of disciplinary procedures follow? That is to say, if we are perforce authori-tarians, how can we become truly effective in our responsibility to promote good discipline? Let me suggest a few principles and their application to the classroom.

Principle 1: Rules should be clear and firm. Rules are the means by which the authoritarian teacher communicates the behavioral standards he deems necessary for the welfare of the class. He should determine unacceptable behaviors and prohibit them by rules for his students. More specifically:

a) Rules should be specific. Classroom rules such as "cooperate with your fellow students," "respect your teacher," or "try hard," lack specificity and may mean widely different things to different students. I once had a teacher who claimed to have only one rule to govern behavior: "be good." We students later figured out the twenty or so specific meanings of that rule by a painful trial-and-error process. So that students do not have to define the real meaning of a rule, state it in specific, objective terms. Such rules as "raise your hand when you have a question," "stay in your seat until the teacher dismisses you," and "keep all scrap paper in your desk until the end of the period" are clear and specific, open to very few interpretations.

b) Rules should be _positive_. Note that in the last examples above students are told what to do, not what _not_ to do. Rules that begin with "don't" invite resistance and often _suggest_ undesirable behaviors. I am reminded of Carl Sandburg's ditty: "We couldn't understand why when we came home from the store the children had beans in their ears. The last thing we told them before we went to the store was _not_ to put beans in their ears." Furthermore, a positive rule suggests the solution to a problem. For example, the positive rule "keep all scrap paper in your desk until the end of the period" lets a student know what to do with the waste paper while the negative rule "don't throw paper" leaves him with the unwanted paper still in his hand.

c) Rules should be _enforced_. No rule means any more than a teacher makes it mean. Indeed, students spend a good deal of time and effort seeing if what a teacher _says_ has anything to do with what he _means_. Consequently, if a teacher wants a rule to be effective, he must demonstrate that the breaking of a rule always has a consequence for the student. This consequence should immediately follow the prohibited behavior and should be consistently applied after any infraction. Enforcement usually is most effective when the consequence is a) logically connected to the offense (e.g., staying after school for coming in to class late) and b) rehabilitative rather than punitive (e.g., washing desk tops for marking up a desk). Rules that are not enforced--quickly, consistently, logically-- might as well not exist. In fact, it is better to eliminate rules you can't or won't enforce because such rules undermine your authority.

Principle 2: Teachers must use action, not anger, to control behavior. Some teachers wear themselves out yelling at students, issuing empty threats, and working themselves into a state of near hysteria--all to no avail. As Dobson asks, "have you ever screamed at your child, 'This is the last time I'm going to tell you this is the last time'?"[5] More specifically:

a) Action should be swift and firm. "Action" implies movement rather than talk; instead of raising your voice and risking a shouting match with a defiant student, it is better to walk over to the student and simply ask him to go with you into the hall for a quick conference. As La Mancusa puts it, "at times of showdowns, it is always wiser to handle the situation with quiet and determined and decisive action. . . . Psychologists would call this action 'therapeutic bouncing.'"[6]

b) The teacher should employ the "soft reprimand" when a student's in-class behavior needs correction. Typically (and naturally) teachers tend to raise their voices when reprimanding a misbehaving student. It's more effective to move toward the student and in a lowered voice to give a specific, quiet, direct command: "Joe, turn around right now and start to work in the assignment." For one thing this approach personalizes a directive; for another, it does not disrupt other students; finally, it is a private communication that does not create a public issue where a student cannot back down because of peer attention.

c) The teacher should be assertive and employ body language to communicate authority. When students are testing a teacher's authority and resolution, it is imperative that the teacher respond effectively. Frederick Jones says, "assertiveness is 95% body language. . . . First turn and face the child. If you aren't willing to commit your body in that direction, don't expect the child to respond. . . . Next, make eye contact. . . . Lean toward him. . . . Very slowly walk up to his desk so your leg is touching it; stand and look at the child. Don't say anything, don't hurry. By that time most kids will fold."[7] Another assertive discipline technique is the "broken record" in which a teacher keeps repeating his request, refusing to be diverted or ignored until the request is obeyed.

Principle 3: Provide structure for the classroom and the lesson. Authoritarians know that students work and learn best in well-organized, directional, and purposeful classrooms. Routines and requirements need to be clear and ordered with understood instructions and boundaries. More specifically:

a) Class should begin with a settling task. Students should be taught routinely when they enter class to begin work on a review drill, a "focusing event" for the new lesson, or a board-work assignment. This initial assignment becomes a control mechanism to focus students on the work at hand. During this quiet-time initial task the teacher can quietly take roll by means of a seating chart. This structure is more effective than the teacher expectation for the students to sit down (with nothing to do!) and be quiet so that the teacher can call the roll.

b) Students should know the objectives and activities planned for the day. It makes no sense to have structure and direction in a lesson but to hide them from the students. If students are told ahead of time what is planned and why it is important and how the objectives will be achieved, they are likely to feel secure and purposeful under your guidance. These plans can be put on the board, the overhead, or a handout. Contracts often serve this purpose well.

c) Classroom environments should reflect the teacher's structure. Seating arrangements, for example, are under the teacher's control. If the lesson is presentational, then traditional rows may suffice. If small-group work is in store, the teacher should make sure that tables or circles are arranged and students are assigned appropriately. At times, the teacher should manipulate lighting, furniture, and time in purposeful ways to contribute to the structural demands of a lesson. Such control communicates the leadership ability of the teacher and inspires respect and confidence from students.

Once teachers are accepted by their students as leaders, as competent instructors, as firm-but-fair disciplinarians who establish clear rules and reasonable structure--then a basis for learning and for freedom within limits exists. Defiance, disruption, and "games students play" become rarities rather than every day, escalating, eroding misadventures. Then--and only then--can teachers begin extending to students an opportunity for shared planning, for negotiated contracts, for full participation in rule-setting and student courts. Then—and only then—can teachers begin the important and meaningful task of democratizing the classroom.

The effective authoritarian establishes his authority only so that he can eventually relinquish his power to students—students who must learn to become responsible citizens of school and society.

FOOTNOTES

1. See, for example, Richard Curwin and Allen Mendler, The Discipline Book: A Complete Guide to School and Classroom Management (Reston, Virginia: Reston Publishing Company, 1980); Charles Wolfgang and Carl Glickman, Solving Discipline Problems: Alternative Strategies for Classroom Teachers (Boston: Allyn and Bacon, 1980); Thomas McDaniel, "Exploring Alternatives to Punishment," Phi Delta Kappan (March, 1980).
2. For a discussion of this issue see my "Corporal Punishment and Teacher Liability: Questions Teachers Ask," The Clearing House (October, 1980), pp. 10-13.
3. Mary Lynn Crow and Merle E. Bonney, "Recognizing the Authoritarian Personality Syndrome in Educators," Phi Delta Kappan (September, 1975), p. 42.
4. Jenny Gray, The Teacher's Survival Guide (Palo Alto, California: Fearon Publishers, 1967), p. 1.
5. James Dobson, Dare to Discipline (Wheaton, Illinois: Tyndale House Publishers, 1970), p. 37.
6. Katherine C. La Mancusa, We Do Not Throw Rocks at the Teacher (Scranton, Pennsylvania: International Textbook Company, 1966), p. 90.
7. Frederick Jones, "Instructor's Guide to Sanity-Saving Discipline," Instructor (November, 1978), p. 64.

A STITCH IN TIME:

PRINCIPLES OF PREVENTIVE DISCIPLINE

School discipline, if we can believe the Gallup Poll, has been the number one problem in American education during the last decade. Many professional articles have dealt with such underlying causes of the problem as permissiveness in today's society, the youth culture and its concomitant alienation, changing values as a result of a changing family structure, frustration among minorities, and a general decline in respect for authority in the post-Vietnam and post-Watergate era. Manifestations of the students' malaise include vandalism, physical and verbal abuse of teachers, cheating and stealing, boredom and indifference, excessive absences and tardiness--and a host of "minor" disruptions (back-talk, clowning, room-wandering, sleeping, etc.) to further complicate the already difficult task of the classroom teacher. So what's a teacher to do?

There are many texts now available to instruct a teacher on how to solve discipline problems, how to handle disruptive students, and how to cope with a degenerating classroom management system. But the key to effective discipline is to <u>prevent</u> problems from developing, festering, and exploding in the classroom. The maxim, "A stitch in time saves nine," has no better application anywhere than in the area of school discipline. Indeed, any approach to discipline--e.g., behavior modification, humanistic psychology, democratic problem-solving will embody principles of prevention. The difficulty is that these principles are often submerged and overpowered by the <u>problems</u> that are under consideration.

Below are a few pragmatic principles of prevention for prudent pedagogues to pursue. They are drawn rather eclectically from various theories and reflect the practices of many effective teachers.

<u>Plan high-interest, purposeful multi-activity lessons</u>.

The purpose of this principle is to prevent the monotony and boredom that often lead to disruption. Every teacher knows that kids who aren't "turned on" by the lesson may turn against the teacher or turn to other diversions. When lessons are student centered, provide variety, and promote active involvement for the students in assigned (and chosen!) tasks, discipline is rarely a problem. This requires a great deal of attention to the planning process. The effective planner knows how to:

·design plans to build on identified student interests and to provide for choice;

·identify the real reasons for activities and assignments;

·include humor and fun in class activities;

·plan several kinds of activities for each lesson;

·plan to ensure individual and small group learning;

·intermix quiet learning (like seat work) with active learning (like games);

·plan transitions between activities, specific questions for specific students, and audio-visual instruction for almost every class;

·experiment with well-planned learning centers, outside projects, and independent research;

·diversify plans to provide for the fast-finisher and the slow learner;

·evaluate and revise plans and involve students in this process. (Cooperative teacher-pupil planning is not nearly so common as it should be.)

The teacher who works hard at the planning phase of instruction--planning the students' learning rather than the teacher's teaching--will prevent many of the causes of poor discipline in the classroom.

Prepare students for your plans.

Motivation is one of the most important pre-requisites for good discipline. Indeed, planning an effective lesson is only part of the teacher's task in preventing boredom and all that derives therefrom. Unless the students are excited by your plans, know

128

your expectations, and share your enthusiasm, the best of plans will fail. To prepare students for various aspects of a lesson, a teacher should be able to:

·make the objectives of a unit, assignment, and lesson clear;

·explain and justify every assignment (and not just by saying, "You'll need this next year.");

·motivate initial learning through "advanced organizers," students' experiences, and inductive techniques;

·move quickly from a motivational technique into the substantive learning, principle, or concept of the lesson;

·make instructions for the completion of the task simple and clear so that there is no confusion or ambiguity about what is expected;

·stimulate curiosity and interest through objects and audio-visual material related to the lesson;

·ask thought-provoking questions that require the students to dig deeper for answers;

·make motivational statements that reflect your own enthusiasm ("I think you are going to find this topic one of the most interesting and valuable issues we could study.");

·use charts and graphs of student progress so that each student can work toward specific goals;

·design home assignments that are interesting extensions and applications of what has been learned in class, reinforcing concepts that have been taught (Not simply, "Do page 45 for homework.").

When a teacher employs the personal approach to motivation in order to prepare students for their involvement and responsibility for learning, students are more likely to be cooperative and task-oriented. When that occurs, you will have eliminated many potential discipline problems.

Predict your potential discipline problems.

Obviously, if you knew how to anticipate, say, a disruption, a confrontation, or a case of cheating, you would be better able to prevent it from happening. And this is precisely what effective preventive discipliners do every day. There is a paradox, however, a teacher needs to be able to anticipate problems but must also expect good behavior, self-fulfilling prophecies being what they are. Preventive discipliners are realistic enough to know that problems and disruptions can indeed occur but are optimistic enough to expect the best from their charges. Predicting potential discipline problems requires that teachers be able to:

·assess motivational problems in students and adjust accordingly;

·identify personality clashes between students and assign seats accordingly;

·read "body language" that suggests a student may be having a bad day;

·plan for "trouble zones" in the day or week: before and after lunch, before holidays, Fridays, rainy days, etc.;

·avoid or limit volatile activities if a class cannot handle the freedom;

·create a time-out area where a disruptive student can cool-off;

·provide quiet times as a means of settling a class;

·use focusing and impoverishing techniques like filmstrips and soft illumination to restrict excessive stimuli;

·greet students as they come into the classroom in the morning, after lunch, or from other activities so that quick anticipatory judgments can be made;

·use verbal and non-verbal cues (and/or switch activities) at the first sign of inattention to nip that behavior in-the-bud. (It helps to know the symptoms, like finger-drumming, eye lid drooping, and window-gazing).

Most discipline problems have symptoms that a wise teacher looks for while at the same time creating the kind of climate and conditions that anticipate and correct for undesirable behavior.

Preserve your dignity and decorum as a model for students.

It is undeniable that teachers teach behavior through example. Children learn behavior and learn it primarily through imitation. Have you ever heard a teacher literally screaming "I want you kids to get quiet right now!"? What do students really learn from such an approach? The teacher who acts the way he or she would have students act can prevent many common classroom disruptions. To model appropriate behavior a teacher should:

·demonstrate a calm, organized, business-like attitude;

·use the "soft reprimand" in a firm but private manner if a student is disruptive;

·talk in a low-volume voice just loud enough to be heard easily in the back of a quiet classroom;

·wait for quiet rather than talking over a rising level of chatter;

·respect the rights of students to be recognized, to express their opinions, to have their needs met;

·engage in silent reading, essay or journal writing, experiments and problem solving (why should kids value such activities if they never see the teacher doing them?);

·be polite (Haim Ginott says treat a student as though he were a guest in your house!);

·be quiet--even tip-toe--when students are quietly working on individual assignments at their desks;

·keep self-control but show students how angry feelings can be expressed through "I-messages." (Not "You delinquents are terrible" but "When you fight I am afraid you will hurt someone and this makes me angry.");

131

be honest, admit mistakes, confess ignorance and in other ways show that teachers are real people.

There are many behaviors--attitudes towards learning, interaction among people, manners--that are caught rather than taught, are learned by osmosis, and depend on the teacher's ability to model these behaviors in the classroom. One way to prevent undesirable behavior is to teach desirable behavior as early as possible, and a positive example has strong instructional consequences.

Praise students for good behavior and for academic success.

If there is one lesson that behavioral psychology has taught teachers it is that positive reinforcement is a powerful shaper of human behavior. All students need attention but many of them find that misbehavior "pays off" handsomely in terms of the attention that results. Even a teacher's hostile reprimands are more rewarding than no attention at all. Whether a teacher is pointing out the mistakes in a student's work or a fault in his behavior, he is emphasizing the negative and reinforcing the very behavior he is trying to correct. To prevent problems with praise, a teacher needs to:

·"catch the child being good" and reward that behavior in some way (Even if Johnny is only in his seat five minutes, chose that time to give him attention and praise);

·ignore minor and non-persisting infractions;

·determine what is rewarding to a class or to the individuals (Use a questionnaire, watch what children do in their free time, ask them to bring in favorite things, etc.);

·set easy-to-reach, short-range goals for behavior and for academic achievement so that success comes easily;

·establish rewards that children will work for;

·explore various token economies for particularly difficult classes;

·keep visible records of progress and give frequent feedback so that students can see their progress;

·expand verbal reinforcers by consciously using alternatives for "good," "right," "O.K." (Be sincere but don't be stingy!);

·expand non-verbal reinforcers like smiles, nods, pats-on-the back, checks for correct answers, special awards;

·experiment with the reward system (Unexpected rewards are often best--think up some five minute "We've been working so well why don't we treat outselves to _____" rewards that you can spring on the class).

A consistent effort to define the behavior you want in your classroom followed by a systematic approach based on positive reinforcement not only sets a positive tone and clear goals for behavior, it teaches students that appropriate behavior is rewarded. It takes work and patience for a teacher to implement such an approach, but the reinforcement principle can be a powerful preventer of discipline problems.

Not even a paragon of pedagogical purity can expect to employ all of these principles of preventive discipline every day and all the time. These are not intended as cookbook recipes; indeed, the application of these principles has been left primarily to the imagination and judgment of the teacher. It is not so much the specific techniques that are at issue here as one's professional attitude. Teachers who want to improve their instruction, the climate in the classroom, and the behavior of their students will succeed if they view the task as one of preventing discipline problems through a well-planned and executed positive approach. Is an ounce of prevention worth a pound of cure? When it comes to classroom discipline, you bet it is!

"WELL BEGUN IS HALF DONE":

A SCHOOL-WIDE PROJECT FOR BETTER DISCIPLINE

Starting the year on the "right foot" is the key to effective classroom discipline. Obviously, of course, naturally--now tell us something new. Well, what's new is that a school can indeed design an inservice beginning-of-the year project that makes a difference in attitudes and actions for teachers, students, and administrators. I want to describe an unusually successful project in school discipline at a small elementary school in Greenwood, South Carolina.

The principal of Mathews Elementary asked me to work with her and her entire staff to establish a better climate, more positive attitudes, and more effective management in a school that draws heavily from a lower socio-economic mill village population. I met with the thirty teachers (and aides) in the late spring to hear their concerns and spent a few minutes in each classroom to get a feel for problems and approaches of teachers. Problems? Student apathy, discourtesy, loudness, fighting, cheating, stealing, classroom chatter--the usual list. Approaches? Teacher-made negative rules, prohibitions, punishments, threats, and yelling--the usual list.

The principal and I decided that we would devote three full morning sessions to working with the staff just prior to the beginning of school in late August to be followed by three days of observation by me as soon as classes began. The three pre-school sessions focused on principles and practices of classroom discipline.

Session One

The first meeting dealt with an overview of theories of discipline. I presented a continuum of discipline strategies to provide a framework and used the concept of "power" to differentiate between theories. The Authoritarian Model (at one extreme) locates power in the role of the teacher and in the administrative offices of the school system. The Behavioral Model locates power in the environment and the contingencies of behavior. The Human Relations

Model (at the other extreme) locates power within the student. And the Pedagogical Model locates power in the interaction between student and teacher, in the dynamics of instruction itself. (See Figure 1)

After examining some of the basic principles and practices that follow from each theory, we gave special attention to the Authoritarian Model, whose premise is that a teacher needs to have good rules, clear and effective consequences for infractions, and "command presence" in the classroom. It is my belief that because schools are in fact (if not theory) authoritarian institutions, teachers need first and foremost to be comfortable with their own authority in the classroom. To illustrate this approach, I showed a movie "Glasser on Discipline," which presents William Glasser outlining his effective program of rule-setting and rule-enforcing techniques. We concluded this session with a rule-setting exercise. Each grade-level group designed three classroom, two hall, and two cafeteria rules that were 1) unambiguous, 2) specific, 3) short, and 4) positive.

Session Two

The next day we went over the homework so that teachers could see the diversity of values and practices they had. We returned briefly to the issue of rules, this time to look at the relationship of rules to punishments and consequences. Teachers measured their collective rules from the day before against the proto-types in Figure 2 and then went to work refining their rules and sequencing consequences for each rule as in the sample one in Figure 2, "students will come to class on time."

Following this phase of training, we turned our attention to the more positive dimension of reinforcement. While clear rules matched with effective consequences can establish proper parameters of authority for the teacher, it is essential that the teacher reward the behavior he or she wants to perpetuate. We discussed the principles of reinforcement (well known to most teachers) and set to work on another small-group exercise to list reinforcers that these teachers could actually use. A simple list was provided to each grade-level group.

136

After generating a master list of concrete, activity, and social reinforcers, we worked on verbal and non-verbal reinforcement practices through a role playing activity. Teachers paired off and took turns going through this four-step exercise:

1. One teacher assumes the role of student, the other the role of teacher.

2. The student raises hand to answer a question from teacher.

3. The teacher says (without looking at the student), "Can you tell me the answer?"

4. When student answers question, teacher says (without emotion), "O.K."

The scenario is repeated, but this time at step #3 the teacher looks at student, smiles, moves toward the student, says "Thank you, Sally, for raising your hand--what is your answer?" At step #4 the teacher nods and gives a specific verbal reinforcer with enthusiasm (such as, "Right on target, Sally; you figured out that addition problem very quickly!").

After both teachers had an opportunity to practice praising, several particularly skillful praisers demonstrated their ability for the rest of the staff.

We concluded this session with some additional modeling exercises, one to show the importance of the teacher using a soft voice while circulating among children doing seat-work and one to show a range of cues teachers and students can use to communicate non-verbally.

Session Three

The final session brought together the rule-enforcement dimension and the positive reinforcement dimension. We viewed another film, this one on "Assertive Discipline in the Classroom" featuring Lee Canter. Canter's emphasis on action by the teacher when a rule is violated--rather than hostility or threats or constant pleading--is especially valuable. His sequence of consequences (name on board as warning, check beside name fifteen minutes after school, two checks beside name call to parents, etc.) gave teachers a concrete system for enforcing rules. The teachers also were intrigued by his use of marbles and a large jar to provide positive reinforcement. He explained to his students that each time he found them working well, behaving well, demonstrating courtesy, raising hands particularly well, etc., he would drop a marble in the jar. Each marble represents fifteen seconds of free time (or whatever reward the teacher deems appropriate) which the students collect when the jar is full (or at the end of the day or week). This can be an effective whole-class token economy.

Next, teachers paired off to role play an assertive discipline technique Canter calls the "broken record." In this exercise (as in the praising exercise) there is a teacher and a student, and roles switch at the end of the first role play:

1. The student engages in disruptive behavior.

2. The teacher says (without looking at the student), "Behave yourself."

3. The teacher looks at student and says, "Behave yourself."

4. The teacher looks at student, points to him and says, "John, I want you to behave."

5. The teacher looks at student, points to him, walks toward him, puts a hand on his shoulder, leans toward him and says, "John, I want you to behave right now."

This is to be done quietly, unemotionally, and firmly. Once students learn that the teacher will indeed follow through with enforcement, testing of limits steadily decreases.

Finally, we practiced some techniques from the Human Relations Model, such as conflict negotiation, effective "I-messages," and problem solving steps (as advocated by Thomas Gordon in Teacher Effectiveness Training). Teachers wrote up on posters their common classroom rules, leaving room for one or two additional regulations as needed by individual teachers, and readied themselves for the first day of school.

Follow-up Observations

During the first three full days of school, I observed in each classroom for a half-hour followed by a twenty to thirty minute conference with the teacher. I designed a special instrument that would permit specific feedback on management and discipline practices we had worked on in the pre-school sessions. (See Figure 4)

Conclusion

The first week of classes at Mathews Elementary astounded us all. Teachers were confident and well organized; students were calm and respectful; the halls were incredibly quiet; and the principal was ecstatic. The exemplary mood may not last indefinitely, but (as the phrase goes) "well begun is half done." The teachers will need to keep working on 1) praising, 2) reinforcing, 3) modeling, 4) cueing, and 5) enforcing. They will need to find new and better reinforcers and to work even harder on motivation. But they know now that their students can be taught to behave properly (and to enjoy the calmer more controlled climate!) and, even more importantly, that as teachers they have the ability to manage and discipline students in a fair, effective, professional way.

Several factors contributed to the overall success of this inservice project. First (and perhaps most important) was the leadership of the principal. Teachers knew from the outset that she initiated the project, was willing to support them, and was going to be an active participant throughout the inservice training. Second was the design of the project. Not only was there a close connection between theory and practice, there was the opportunity for each teacher to get prepared--with rules, consequences, enforcement techniques, positive reinforcement techniques, etc.--to begin the school year with a program of preventive discipline. Establishing the proper setting events (both time and place) was a crucial element in the success of the project. Third was school-wide consensus on discipline policies and practices. As teachers worked together, they created a unified and mutually supportive approach to the school's discipline problems.

In the process the teachers, aides, and principal developed an esprit de corps and positive attitudes that gave them a new confidence and a new enthusiasm for the difficult job of educating the young. The principal plans to relieve each teacher for a while each month so that a peer observation system can be developed to perpetuate the early success of this project. And who knows where that may lead? Out of such acorns have mighty oak trees grown.

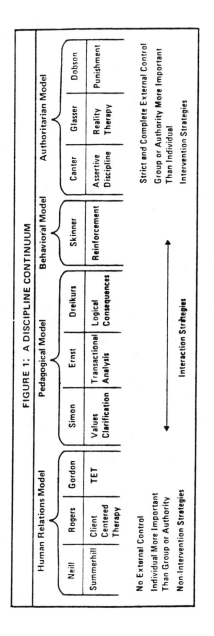

FIGURE 1: A DISCIPLINE CONTINUUM

Human Relations Model		Pedagogical Model			Behavioral Model	Authoritarian Model		
Neill	Rogers	Gordon	Simon	Ernst	Dreikurs	Skinner	Canter	Glasser	Dobson
Summerhill	Client Centered Therapy	TET	Values Clarification	Transactional Analysis	Logical Consequences	Reinforcement	Assertive Discipline	Reality Therapy	Punishment

No External Control

Individual More Important
Than Group or Authority

Non-Intervention Strategies

Interaction Strategies

Strict and Complete External Control

Group or Authority More Important
Than Individual

Intervention Strategies

141

FIGURE 2

POOR RULES	GOOD RULES	BETTER RULES	PUNISHMENTS	CONSEQUENCES
1. be good	1. don't throw paper on floor	1. keep scrap paper at your desk	1. go to principal	1. clean up
2. try hard	2. don't leave assignments undone	2. complete all assignments	2. teacher lecture	2. stay in after school to finish
3. cooperate	3. don't talk while the teacher is talking	3. raise your hand when you want to talk	3. detention	3. teacher ignores contribution
4. respect one another	4. don't hit classmates	4. settle arguments by discussion	4. paddling	4. time out

CONSEQUENCES

1. a) make up time after school
   b) detention
   c) loss of free time privileges
   d) parent conference with teacher/administrator
   e) any student who is always on time may _____

RULE:

1. students will come to class on time
2. students will stay in seats unless given permission to get up
3. students will work quietly during tests

142

FIGURE 3

DISCIPLINE AND MANAGEMENT EVALUATION FORM

TEACHER _____ CLASS _____ DATE _____

	SUPERIOR	SATISFACTORY	NEEDS IMPROVEMENT
A. PLANNING/PREVENTION			
1. Room and materials ready			
2. Objectives made clear to students			
3. Variety of activities prepared			
4. Involvement and application planned			
5. Rules for conduct clear			
6. Structure of lesson clear			
7. Motivation provided			

COMMENT:

	SUPERIOR	SATISFACTORY	NEEDS IMPROVEMENT
B. EXECUTION/ACTION			
1. Lesson begins promptly			
2. Knowledge conveyed with confidence			
3. Disruptions observed and handled quickly and firmly			
4. Expectations for behavior communicated clearly and authoritatively			
5. Verbal correction (firm but non-punitive)			
6. Non-verbal correction (gestures, proximity)			
7. Private correction (soft reprimand)			
8. Pacing of lesson			
9. Reinforcement of behavior			
10. Follow-through/ consequences for misbehavior			
11. Transitions			
12. Closing class			

COMMENT:

	SUPERIOR	SATISFACTORY	NEEDS IMPROVEMENT
C. PERSONAL STYLE/RAPPORT			
1. Assertiveness/command presence			
2. Movement			
3. Energy level			
4. Modeling (courtesy/quiet)			
5. Radar			
6. With-itness			
7. Friendliness/positive attitude			
8. Sensitivity to AGMs			
9. Fairness			

COMMENT:

ABOUT THE AUTHOR

THOMAS R. McDANIEL, a native of Herndon, Virginia, is professor of education, Head of the Division of Education, and Director of the Master of Education Program at Converse College, Spartanburg, South Carolina. He received his undergraduate training at Hampden-Sydney College where he graduated magna cum laude with majors in English and psychology. He earned the MAT (English), MLA (Humanities), and Ph.D. (Education) from The Johns Hopkins University, specializing in administration and philosophy in his doctoral work. Prior to his appointment at Converse in 1971, he taught English and Latin in public and private schools and served for seven years as Assistant and Associate Director of the MAT program, Supervisor of Interns, and Instructor in Micro-teaching at Johns Hopkins. His honors include Phi Beta Kappa, Omicron Delta Kappa, Psi Chi, Gamma Sigma, Sigma Upsilon, Alpha Psi Omega, Eta Sigma Phi, Pi Gamma Mu, Phi Sigma Pi, and Who's Who Among Students in American Universities and Colleges. Professor McDaniel has served on the Spartanburg County Board of Education (Chairman), The South Carolina Society for the Study of the Foundations of Education (President), the Board of Directors of The Charles Lea Center (Chairman), and on many other boards and committees. Professional journals have published over fifty of his articles, essays, and reviews, and his work has been included in such anthologies as The Cream of the Kappan 1956-81, and Kaleidoscope: Readings in Education (1980). He has also written a textbook chapter for The Reality of Teaching (Kendall/Hunt) and has given dozens of workshops and speeches locally and nationally on such topics as school law and school discipline. University Press of America published his text The Teacher's Profession in 1982. Dr. McDaniel resides in Spartanburg with his wife Nan and his children Robb and Katy.